Reserve

HOME
BREW

THE ULTIMATE GUIDE TO MAKING YOUR OWN TIPPLE

DOUG ROUXEL AND SARA PASTON-WILLIAMS

PAVILION

CONTENTS

INTRODUCTION

Whether you have a glut of produce on the allotment, an abundance of apples on your apple tree or simply a burning desire to create your own brew, *Home Brew* is the much needed, one-stop guide to everything you need to know about making your own drinks. Avoid the disasters, the exploding bottles in the airing cupboard, the ever-so-slightly flat brews, the over-sweetened sloe gins, and take advantage of our collection of tried and tested recipes that will impress even the most discerning drinker.

The recipes come with variations set to inspire you, information on how to get started and also a comprehensive guide to all the skills, techniques and processes involved in making your own brew. Armed with this knowledge, the world of fruit wines, beers, ciders, spirits and cordials is really at your fingertips.

Have fun creating brews for many occasions. Fruity cordials make a thirst-quenching offering for a barbecue, light and refreshing elderflower or lavender champagnes add a special touch to any celebration, and a bottle of sloe gin or quince brandy can solve your Christmas present conundrums.

This resource is not meant to be precious, so we've already stained the pages for you! Be free, feel inspired and enjoy making your own tipple without boundaries.

Cheers!

PART ONE
GETTING STARTED

THE BASICS

all you need to know

UNDERSTANDING THE BASICS

HOW ARE ALCOHOLIC DRINKS MADE?

This chapter is about the basic principles of making many kinds of alcoholic drinks. It covers the essential areas that are common to all of them, no matter which drink specifically interests you. It takes you through the preparation needed, explains how the sugars are obtained, how the process of fermentation works and how long it takes for this to become something drinkable.

The terms 'brew' and 'brewing' are often used, which might seem slightly 'beer-centric'. It's not intended to be: there just isn't a better catch-all term.

DEALING WITH FUNGI AND BACTERIA

The central process to home brewing – or, in fact, any brewing – is fermentation. This promotes the growth of yeast, a fungus, in order for it to work through its lifecycle in our brew, so that we end up with an alcoholic drink. Creating ideal conditions for a fungus to thrive, though, means that we are making conditions that will enable many other fungi and bacteria to thrive too. So keeping things clean and sanitary is of paramount importance.

In order that our desired fungus (the brewing yeast) has the greatest chance to gain full control of our brew, and that unwanted micro-organisms (wild yeasts or vinegar bacteria, for example) have little or no chance of procreation, we must ensure that things are not only clean but also sterilized.

Within home brewing terminology, 'sterilizing' is the term most often used. However, it is not strictly a sterilizing process: we do not want to kill all bacteria; we just want to ensure that our bacteria has the best chance of surviving. 'Sanitizing' would possibly be a better term, but 'sterilizing' is widely accepted and understood.

CLEANING

All equipment used in the brewing process must be cleaned and, as much as possible, all marks and discolouration removed. Household detergents such as washing-up liquid can be used, but more stubborn stains may require the use of soda crystals. Glass is easy to clean and does not stain readily, which made it the mainstay of home brewing for many years. The expense of large glass vessels has seen its popularity decrease in favour of food-grade plastic, but these are more difficult to keep clean. Some shapes of container are more difficult to clean (bottles and demi-johns, for example) and may require a specially shaped brush to reach the corners. These can be obtained from good home-brewing suppliers.

Once all the items in the brewing process have been cleaned, they must be fully rinsed. This is to ensure that all residues of detergent are removed. Detergents in the finished products may spoil the taste. They affect beer in particular, altering the surface tension of the beer, meaning that it will not maintain a head.

STERILIZATION

All equipment that comes into contact with the brew prior to or following the fermentation process requires sterilizing. If there is any lengthy boiling that takes place in the brewing process (for full-mash beers, for example), anything that comes into contact before the boil must be clean but does not require sterilizing. Anything that comes into contact with the brew *after* the boil will, of course, require sterilizing.

The main sterilizing solutions used in home brewing are chlorine-based. The easiest way to ensure the correct volume and strength of solution is to use one of the many home-brewing cleaning and sterilizing solutions available from any home brew supplier.

It is possible to use simple household bleach, calculating the volume to create a solution of an appropriate strength, but this is not an approach we would recommend for a beginner.

Sterilization is also important in winemaking. Airborne yeasts and vinegar bacteria can only be kept at bay by constant vigilance. 'Sulphite' is described as the winemaker's best friend. This is most commonly available in the form of Campden tablets, but can also be bought as a crystalline powder called sodium or potassium metabisulphite.

Make a solution of one Campden tablet, a few grains of citric acid (see page 27) and 600ml/ 1 pint/2½ cups cold water. Use to rinse all your equipment, before and after use, to sterilize it.

This has the advantage of being a solution that is less likely to taint the flavour of the final drink. However, the level of sanitization it offers is below that of the modern chlorine-based cleaners and, as such, it has fallen from favour with home brewers.

EXTRACTING SUGARS

The fermentation process central to the brewing process requires sugar. Generally, alcoholic drinks are most notable in difference due to the different sources of sugar used in their creation. The extraction of these sugars is, in many cases, a central part in the process, although in some types of brewing, notably when making mead or brewing from kits, the sugars come from honey, grape concentrate or malt extract, which are very easy to mix into a liquid.

To make most wines and ciders, the sugars are extracted from the fruit by a combination of crushing and pressing. In many 'country wines', the sugars from the fruit are bolstered by the addition of household sugar to maintain the alcohol level and taste balance found in grape wines.

The most complex sugar extraction process that the home brewer is likely to encounter is the one used for full-mash beers. In this process, the crushed, malted grains are 'mashed' to promote a chemical reaction that releases the sugars from the grain. These are then washed from the grains during sparging (see page 54).

Fermentable sugars are commonly used in the brewing process. These are sugars that can be readily converted by the yeast into alcohol, but there are many sugars that are not fermentable.

These are not used in great quantities in home brewing, though they have an important place in some styles of drinks. A good example is a sparkling but sweet cider; this would either require forced carbonation, or the addition of an unfermentable sugar to allow unchecked fermentation at the end of the process, so creating the fizz but retaining the desired level of sweetness. Another example is milk stout, a sweeter but fizzy style of beer containing lactose (an unfermentable sugar found in milk); without the unfermentable sugar, the sweetness would disappear in the carbonation process. Sucralose is a widely available non-fermentable sweetener, commercially known as Splenda.

FERMENTATION

Once you have followed the instructions given for the sterilizer, it is very important (unless otherwise advised by the product instructions) to fully rinse the sterilizing solution off the brewing equipment. This should be done with cold water directly from the tap, at least once. (When using chlorine-based sanitizers, a good sniff of the equipment should indicate how much rinsing is required.) The rinsing will ensure that there are no chemicals left on the equipment which might taint the taste of the final product.

Once the sugars have been extracted and combined with water to create must (winemaking) or wort (beer-making), the next step in the process is to ferment them. Fermentation is the process that gives a drink its alcoholic kick. The fermentation process is slightly different for different drinks and, more importantly, for types of yeast. However, there are a number of factors common to almost all brewing processes.

In the initial stages of fermentation, the yeast multiplies rapidly. This is very important as the number of yeast cells added to start fermentation is generally quite small, and a much larger number are required to complete the fermentation. The multiplication process is aerobic – that is, the yeast requires oxygen to be available to it.

For some wines and when brewing from kits, less boiling takes place (and, in some cases, there is a lot of activity crushing and mashing and extracting juice from fruit), which means that there will be sufficient oxygen to allow this element of the ferment to take place. However, in beers that are fully boiled, much of the oxygen will be removed, so the beer will have to be aerated (more oxygen added) to make the yeast multiply.

Once the yeast has completed its rapid multiplication, the main phase of the ferment will begin. In this part, the yeast will be working anaerobically – i.e. surviving without oxygen. The yeast will start to work on the available sugars: in the simplest terms, it begins breaking them down and eventually turns them into alcohols and carbon dioxide (CO_2). The simplest sugars are broken down first. Some sugars are too complex for the yeast to break down itself, and it will create an enzyme that breaks down the sugars into something the yeast can then process. This is the reason why non-natural sugars, like sucralose, cannot be broken down by yeast, as there is no enzyme that will help to break it down.

The final phase of the process is the clean-up. While converting sugars to alcohol and CO_2, the yeasts also create by-products. The final process the yeast undertakes is to break these down. This is important in some styles that require a clean, fresh taste (like European lagers) and can also be part of the style (like an Extra Special Bitter). The clean-up process usually takes place at the conclusion of the vigorous fermentation and can be helped by leaving the brew to sit for a couple of days after the fermentation has finished.

Should fermentation take place in the open or be enclosed in a container? There are many schools of thought, particularly with respect to beers. Indeed, some beers rely on being left in the open, to be fermented by wild yeasts. In general, it is easiest to enclose the brew with a stopper or lid. This must be done in such a way that CO_2 is able to escape from the brew. This release of CO_2 is often done via an airlock – either in a hole in the lid of a bucket, or pushed into a hole in a stopper in the neck of a demi-john. For more details, see Fermentation/Maturation Containers on page 19.

MAINTAINING THE TEMPERATURE

For the reactions to occur as expected, the ideal temperature for the particular strain of yeast must be maintained. Some yeasts – most wine and 'ale' yeasts, in fact – require fermentation at 20/21°C (68–70°F). However, some yeasts – notably lager yeasts – require a lower temperature. Temperature control is an important element in fermentation: too low, and it will come to a standstill, leaving you with a sweet, non-alcoholic drink; too high, and the speed will increase, creating additional by-products that add 'off' flavours to the final product. It is important to know the ideal temperature range for the yeast you are using, and to maintain the temperature of the ferment at that level. This is easy enough when the yeast requires temperatures in the range at which we tend to keep our houses. However, if you are brewing in a garage, or require a lower temperature, some kind of system will be required to regulate the temperature.

Home brew suppliers sell a number of heater systems, including a brew belt or the mat heaters normally used in aquaria and vivaria, which will raise the temperature. Some home brewers use a refrigerator to keep the temperature cool – a particular issue in summer. Control systems (as used for aquaria) are available, which switch heaters and coolers on and off, thus maintaining the temperature in the acceptable range. If you intend to brew lager regularly, or live in a region with hot summers, this is probably essential.

DIFFERENT TYPES OF YEAST

There are many types of yeast and they differ in many ways. Some work at the top of the body of liquid, some at the bottom; some form hard deposits of dead yeast in the bottom of the vessel, some are loose; some impart little to the taste of a brew, some have obvious taste profiles. There are some all-purpose yeasts, which work well across a variety of styles, and there are some yeasts that are specific to a particular style. This is an area open to experimentation.

MONITORING FERMENTATION

To track the rate of fermentation, and to identify when it has finished, there are various observations to note and measurements to take. First, look at the surface: in the early stages of fermentation, there will be a froth on the surface. If the fermenter is see-through, you will see bubbles rising; if it is not, you can often see the bubbles reaching the surface. This gives an indication of the vigour of the ferment, but for a more accurate picture, a hydrometer is required.

This is an instrument for measuring the weight, or sugar content, of a liquid and is by far the most important piece of equipment for the winemaker or home brewer. It shows how much sugar remains in the solution, enabling you to calculate how much has been used in fermentation. This lets you determine the alcohol content, as well as how sweet or dry the end product will be.

Alcohol not only contributes to the taste of a drink, it preserves it as well. Wines with an alcohol content of less than 10% may not keep well; wines above 14% might need to carry a health warning!

A hydrometer is a simple piece of equipment – a float with a long, thin neck that sticks out of the liquid, a weight at the bottom to make it sit upright, and a scale marked on it to show how deep in the liquid it is sitting. The hydrometer indicates the amount of sugar left, and it does this by bobbing about in the liquid. (Make sure the hydrometer is floating freely, and is not touching the sides of the container.) The more sugar there is, the higher the hydrometer will sit in the liquid. As the yeast turns the sugar into alcohol, the liquid thins and the hydrometer will sit lower in it.

Hydrometers are cylindrical and made of glass, with a knack of finding the best way to roll off a worktop or out of a cupboard and on to the floor – to smash. So keep a spare, just in case.

The measurement taken with a hydrometer is called the specific gravity (or 'gravity'). It is normal to take a reading and record it before the yeast goes in (Original Gravity, or OG) and at the end (Final Gravity, or FG). Gravity readings are recorded as a number, written as 1046 or 1.046; in some cases just the last two numbers are referenced (*i.e.* 46). The specific gravity of plain water is 1000 (or 1.000 or 00). However, this will change as the temperature changes, so it is important to ensure that the liquid is at the exact temperature your hydrometer is calibrated for (normally 15°C or 20°C/59°F or 68°F) or use a temperature correction chart to work out the offset introduced by the temperature difference.

When taking a gravity reading, it is good practice to draw off a small amount to be tested into a sterilized trial jar, and then take the reading from there. This ensures an accurate reading: you should be at eye level to the surface, and be able to see the meniscus that forms around the hydrometer (the liquid will be drawn slightly up the sides) but which slightly obscures the reading unless you are level with it.

You can take gravity readings every day if you wish, but it's most important to measure the gravity towards the end of the fermentation (7–10 days normally).

Once the gravity reading remains the same for a full 24-hour period, and is near the final gravity quoted for the recipe, style, or, in the case of wines and ciders, preferred dryness, the initial fermentation has finished.

At the end of fermentation, a wine may have an SG of slightly less than pure water – 990–996 is typical of a dry wine. For medium wines, it may be 996–1009 and for sweet ones, 1009–1018.

Since sweet wines require a little sugar at the end of fermentation, start with a higher SG of perhaps 1100 to ensure you have the same amount of alcohol at the end – though this will depend on how tolerant the yeast is to alcohol.

ONCE FERMENTATION STOPS

Once the initial vigorous fermentation has stopped, it is possible to stop further fermentation – and therefore further consumption of sugars – to ensure the brew remains still and at the same level of sweetness. To stabilize it, simply add Campden tablets. Add one tablet per 4.5 litres/1 gallon/4¾ quarts at the end of the initial fermentation.

Gravity readings enable us to calculate the alcohol by volume, or ABV – something of interest to many brewers. It is easy enough to calculate what this is – as set out below, using 7.36 to represent the relationship between the amount of sugars consumed in the multiplication of the yeast, and those consumed in the creation of alcohol. Some more complex formulae have different constants for different OG levels, but for simplicity there is a single constant in this case.

OG (original gravity)	1047
FG (final gravity)	1012
Drop in gravity	35 points
ABV	35/7.36 = 4.7%

As previously discussed, not all yeasts are created equal, and different yeasts are chosen for their different qualities. One of the qualities considered is the level of expected attenuation of the yeast. This is expressed as a percentage and gives an indication of the percentage of sugars that will be consumed by the yeast during fermentation.

RACKING

This is the process of transferring a brew from one container to another. Once the fermentation has taken place, it is very important to ensure that little or no further oxygen is added because this can taint the taste and is also a primary reason why a drink may go off. It is also important to leave behind the sediment (known as the 'trub' in beers or 'lees' in wines). This can taint the taste of a brew, so racking the brew off the sediment is an important skill for any home brewer.

The simplest way of doing this is to use a siphon, a length of hose that will reach from the full vessel to the empty vessel. These should be at different heights, with the full container at the top and the empty one below. The greater the difference in height, the quicker the process will be. When using a simple tube, suck on one end until the liquid runs down and then leave it to run from one vessel to the other.

This process can be fiddly, particularly if you are bottling, and a couple of bits of equipment will help. The first is a solid plastic tube with an upturned cap on it. This helps to stop sediment making its way into the siphon and also helps to hold the siphon to the side of the brewing vessel.

Also useful is a racking cane, a solid piece of tubing on the other end of the siphon. It has a needle valve that will allow flow-through when pushed on to the base of a vessel, and will halt the flow when lifted off. This makes bottling much easier, and means you don't have to suck on the siphon tube.

Instead of sucking on the siphon tube, you can fill the siphon completely with tap water and then put one end in the brew. Open the bottom of the siphon (just press on the base of the vessel with a racking cane) and let the water run out into a waste-collecting vessel. Once the beer or wine starts running through, stop the siphon by closing the valve (or lifting the cane) and transfer the siphon to the desired container. To make life easier, use an auto-siphon, with an in-built pump.

CONDITIONING

Even when the fermentation has finished, the drink is not ready. Many of the flavours associated with red wine and several styles of beer come from the conditioning process. The depth of flavour of wines is not immediate, and in beers the hop profile is harsh, mellowing over time. This is the area in which a home brewer has an advantage over a commercial brewer. Storing beer for any time costs money, so ageing attracts a premium, or the beer is left for the minimum amount of time. Only a small minority of commercial brewers mature their beer for any length of time. As home brewers, the only criterion is our own self-control (or lack of it – mine is very poor, and I end up drinking brews earlier than I should).

HOW LONG DO I NEED TO WAIT?

The time it takes to condition a brew will differ between drinks. As a general rule, certainly for beers, every 10 points of gravity above 1000 equate to 1 week of conditioning. In our example brew, which had an OG of 1047 – which is 47 above 1000, so, the conditioning should be 4–5 weeks minimum. Weaker beers, below 5% ABV, will keep for around 3 months in the right conditions, and stronger beers will keep longer.

Conditioning wine is a very different process, and can take significantly longer. The higher alcohol content in wine means that it will keep much longer. Many wines are drinkable within 6–9 months, but most will benefit from 12 or more months conditioning/maturing. If longer is required, the recipe will state as much.

WHERE SHOULD I LEAVE IT?

For the conditioning process, there are optimum conditions: somewhere cool (broadly 15–18°C/ 59–65°F, but lower for some styles), which stays at a constant temperature, and is out of the light. Light can ruin the colour of wine and kill the flavours in beer. A good way of maintaining the temperature is to mature in bulk, as larger volumes take more time to vary in temperature. Rather than bottling before you mature, rack from your fermenter into a demi-john or appropriate container and mature there. This works well for still drinks that do not need conditioning and maturing to create fizz. If space and equipment do not permit bulk conditioning, mature in the bottle, but keep a close eye on the temperature.

STORAGE

It is not always practical or possible to store a brew in a large container, and certainly a demi-john is not the ideal way to serve your brews. Some home brewers are put off bottling, particularly beer brewers, since it requires the cleaning and sterilization of 40 or more bottles. The other option for beer is kegging – this is covered in the beer section.

GENERAL EQUIPMENT

The equipment needed for making wine and beer is quite simple and inexpensive. For equipment specific to beer-making, see page 40.

FERMENTATION/MATURATION CONTAINERS

The type of fermentation vessel is basically chosen by size more than anything else. For a large brew your easiest choice is a high-density polythene, food-grade plastic brewing bucket; these come in sizes 4.5 litres/1 gallon/4¾ quarts up to 30 litres/ 6½ gallons/8 US gallons in volume. They are cheap, easy to clean and store, and light to handle; but always buy white, high-density plastic or polythene – not black, low-grade plastic. In the United States, a carboy is more common; this is similar to a demi-john but in a much larger size. More exotic fermenters are available: for beer brewing on a slightly larger scale, conical fermenters are used, which allow the dead yeast (or trub) to settle in the bottom of the upturned cone so that it can be removed without disturbing the brew itself.

When making beer, cider, perry or mead, you will only need one fermenter, although having two is very useful; for winemaking, you need at least two. For wines, you need one lidded bucket for the first soaking of the fruit, flowers or vegetables, and one for the first stage of fermentation. The lid keeps out foreign matter, but also excludes the vinegar fly, which can turn an entire batch of wine into vinegar.

Beer, cider and perry can all be fermented, then matured in the bottle or keg. However because wines and meads require an initial fermentation then a secondary fermentation and they are easier to mature in bulk, at least two containers are required.

If you are making a 6 bottle, approximately 4.5 litres/1 gallon/4¾ quarts, batch of wine or mead, for secondary fermentation and maturing you will need at least two glass or plastic 4.5 litres/ 1 gallon/4¾ quarts demi-johns. The brew can then be transferred (racked) between the two containers throughout the secondary fermentation and stored for maturation. (The wine or mead will occupy these for several months, so buy more if you wish to make another batch immediately.)

For each demi-john you buy, you will also need one single-holed rubber bung and a glass or plastic 'fermentation lock'. This must be inserted in the rubber bung of the fermentation jar and half-filled with a sulphite solution to create an air-tight seal and keep out the vinegar fly.

The fermentation lock also indicates when fermentation has finished because the bubbles formed by the carbon dioxide given off during fermentation eventually stop.

A supply of tight-fitting, solid bungs to seal the demi-johns during maturation is essential.

HYDROMETER
For measuring the sugar content (see page 30–31).

TEMPERATURE CONTROL SYSTEMS
To maintain the temperature when brewing beer (see page 15, 41–42).

SIPHON AND RACKING CANE
For racking (see page 31).

NYLON SIEVE, NYLON BAG AND PLASTIC FUNNEL
At several stages during winemaking it will be necessary to strain the liquor. Use a nylon sieve for coarse-straining and a nylon jelly bag for straining out the finer particles in the later stages. Don't use a metal sieve, which will impart a metallic taste to the wine. You will also need a white polythene funnel, about 12½cm/5in in diameter, for filling the demi-johns.

LARGE WOODEN OR PLASTIC SPOON AND MASHER (OR BREWER'S PADDLE)
Keep a large, long-handled, non-metallic spoon and vegetable masher solely for brewing. If used for other purposes, they may transfer unwanted tastes to the wine. Do not use metal utensils, since metal readily absorbs undesirable flavours.

The spoon may also be known as a brewer's paddle when making beer.

LITMUS PAPER
For testing the acidity of wine (see page 30).

BOTTLES
Bottles are convenient and allow for the easy transport and consumption of smaller amounts of drink than a keg. Dark glass is preferable: dark green for red wines and brown for beers. Light-coloured drinks such as white wine can go in lighter or clear bottles. Home-brewed beer must be stored in brown bottles, as sunlight can convert some of the compounds in the hop flavouring to something similar to the chemical used by skunks to scare predators – not to be recommended! The colour of red wine can be significantly changed by sunlight, and a dark green bottle will help combat this. You can, of course, store clear glass bottles in a cupboard, out of sunlight. If recycling bottles from the supermarket, do not use bottles that contained spirits: these are made of thinner glass.

Plastic bottles are cheap and easy to obtain, but few good-quality alcoholic drinks are sold in these because they are made of PET plastic, which allows oxygen into the brew, meaning that it will go stale quickly. They are okay for short-term storage, but nothing longer than a month or two. Some plastic bottles are sold with a nylon liner, which can help. Personally, I prefer glass: it's an aesthetic thing, I suppose.

NYLON BOTTLE BRUSHES
A large brush is useful to clean out the fermentation jars, and a smaller brush for cleaning bottles.

CORKS, CAPS AND STOPPERS
Anything you use to close the bottles must be sterilized – something that can be overlooked.

Corks must be soaked in a sulphite solution for several hours until soft and sterilized, before being put into the bottle.

The type of bottles you have will dictate the closure you use: wine bottles generally have corks and beer bottles crown caps, although some beer bottles have swingtops, which are convenient to use and can be reused.

Crown caps open easily and are not an expensive outlay. A good crown capper tool is a necessity. The small all-plastic ones are effective on easy-to-cap bottles. A large, handheld metal one or, even better, a bench capper will cap almost any type of bottle. I tend to hold them with my knees and use both hands on the capper.

Corks – whether plastic or made of cork – are a more complex issue, as there are more varieties available. Some plastic corks can be reused, but do check with the manufacturer or an experienced brewer. Of course, if you use a corkscrew to remove a cork it cannot be reused. Real corks require a corking device, also known as a flogger. Generally, straight-sided corks are preferred for the long term because they ensure a better seal on the bottle than tapered, or flanged, corks that are pressed into the bottle by hand. Bottles with real cork closures will need to be stored sideways so that the cork is kept moist; if they dry out, air can get in, and be difficult to remove. As a final touch, buy 'shrink capsules' to place over the cork once it is in the bottle. These are then heated with a hairdryer to form an extra seal.

LABELS
Two kinds of labels will be useful – a large tie-on label for attaching to buckets and fermentation jars, to record the progress of the fermentation, and stick-on labels for the finished bottles.

MAKING FRUIT WINES AND SPIRITS

the essential information

THE BASIC PRINCIPLES

Winemaking is one of the oldest crafts known to humanity. It relies on the fact that when sugar and yeast are brought together under the right conditions, they can produce alcohol and carbon dioxide. The latter floats off into the atmosphere, while the alcohol remains in the liquid to produce an alcoholic beverage.

Although 'wine' is defined in the dictionary firstly as the fermented juice of the grape, its second definition is as fermented liquor made from the juice of other fruits, flowers and herbs. Herbs, flowers and garden fruits such as cherries, redcurrants, wild elderberries and blackberries, were first used to make wine in the late seventeenth century, when sugar became cheaper and more available.

Making your own wine can be a fascinating hobby and the equipment is simple and cheap, as are the ingredients. But a certain amount of care and attention to detail is necessary to ensure good results, so I suggest you aim to make 4.5 litres/1 gallon/4¾ quarts of a single type in the first year, rather than trying to make a large number in rapid succession and finding that you end up with a number of curiously flavoured vinegars! A simple wine such as blackberry is a good one to start with, as it is excellent either dry or sweet.

The important things to remember are that all your equipment must be sterilized and the wine must be kept covered at every stage to avoid contamination by organisms such as the vinegar fly, which appears as if by magic around any fermenting liquor or fruit. This tiny fly is the winemaker's biggest enemy. Instead of turning to alcohol, your liquor will turn to vinegar, and you will have the sad job of pouring it all down the sink.

The other piece of advice is to try and resist the urge to open your wine too soon. None will be ready to drink in much under 6 months from the time you start – most will need a good deal longer to mature.

THE INGREDIENTS

Home-made wines have four main ingredients: **flavouring, water, sugar and yeast.** Other things play a part, notably acids, tannin and substances that nourish the yeast and, of course, an important element is time (for maturation).

FLAVOURING

The best wine is usually prepared from the best ingredients. This doesn't mean the most expensive, though: surplus fruits and vegetables make good wine as long as they have been freshly picked. Items that you would normally throw away, such as peapods, also make excellent wine as long as they are young and fresh. The countryside is full of flowers, fruit and berries from early spring to late autumn and make the most delectable wines.

Cooking varieties of fruit tend to give the best results. Often, the flavour of a fruit is increased when it is made into wine. This is especially true for gooseberries, strawberries and raspberries.

WATER

Unfortified wine is 80–85 per cent water, so it's lucky for the amateur winemaker that ordinary tap water is suitable for making wine. What's more, the quality of wine is less dependent than is beer on the water used to make it. Excessive chlorination in domestic tap water does ruin its flavour, but there is a simple remedy: boil the water. Don't use distilled water: it lacks the oxygen and the trace elements that yeast needs. Fermentation begins, but stops and cannot be restarted. Cold water is recommended for use with some fruits, such as apples and quinces, and for flower wines. Usually, boiling water is poured over the ingredients to make the must. This not only assists with its purification, but also softens the skin and flesh.

SUGAR

Ordinary white, granulated (beet or cane) sugar is best for making wine. Cheap to buy and without flavour, it can be used in crystal form or dissolved in hot water to form a syrup, then brought to the boil to ensure sterility. Brown sugar – such as demerara – will add a flavour of caramel or burnt sugar and is not recommended for delicate white wines.

YEAST

Of the main ingredients in winemaking, yeast is the most important. The ideal conditions for it to work best are a sugary, slightly acid solution, with certain other yeast nutrients present and a favourable temperature (18–24°C/65–75°F). Many special wine yeasts are available, cultured from yeast cells taken from grapes grown in wine-producing regions. Often a specific type – such as Bordeaux, Hock, and Champagne – these yeasts are better and more reliable than bakers' and brewers' yeasts. Granulated wine yeasts are sold in sachets and usually have nutrient salts added to provide the right amount of nourishment for the yeast, ensuring good fermentation. Both yeast and yeast nutrient can be bought separately if you wish.

OTHER ESSENTIALS
CITRIC ACID
Lack of acidity in a wine leads to 'stuck' fermentation, dullness and a medicinal off-flavour. Check acidity by tasting, or use litmus papers (see page 30). Many fruits contain plenty of acid naturally, so no more needs to be added, but flowers and vegetables contain very little, so acid must be added.

Citric acid, the main acid in all citrus fruits, is the best to add to wine. It promotes rapid and thorough fermentation, has a pleasant taste and is cheap. Oranges and lemons are used instead of citric acid crystals, if their flavour is required.

PRECIPITATE OF CHALK
Some fruits, such as rhubarb, contain too much acid. Some of this can be removed by adding precipitate of chalk.

YEAST NUTRIENT
The yeast cell needs nitrogen as well as oxygen to enable it to grow and thrive. Yeast nutrient, added to the must with the yeast, ensures a steady growth which is essential during fermentation.

TANNIN
Tannin occurs naturally in the skins of many fruits and berries, especially red ones, and in their stones and stalks. It gives character to a wine and is valuable as a preservative and as an aid to clearing and maturation. Lack of tannin ranks

with lack of acid as the most common winemaking fault.

More often than not, it will be necessary to buy wine tannin powder (made from grape skins and stalks) and add it to the must with the yeast and yeast nutrient. Mix the recommended amount into a paste with a little of the must and stir into the rest – ½ teaspoon is usually enough for 4.5 litres/1 gallon/4¾ quarts of liquor.

PECTIN-DESTROYING ENZYME
Many fruits, especially stone fruits such as apricots and plums, and root vegetables like parsnips, contain a lot of pectin. This forms a jelly when boiled with sugar – the setting factor in jam-making. This must be avoided in winemaking because it makes the juices more difficult to extract and can also cause the wine to remain stubbornly cloudy, or develop a 'pectin haze'.

Most winemakers add a small quantity of a pectin-destroying enzyme to the must as a matter of course. It can be bought under various trade names such as Pectinol and Pectolase. Use as directed on the packet. It is best added to the must during the steeping process when the liquor is lukewarm, and 1–2 days before the sugar and yeast are added. It is a good habit to add a pectin-destroying enzyme at the same time as a Campden tablet.

CAMPDEN TABLETS
Campden tablets prevent the growth of bacteria and mould in must and finished wine. Add one Campden tablet per 4.5 litres/1 gallon/4¾ quarts, right at the start of steeping the must. Do not add yeast for at least 24 hours, or it will be inhibited. The addition of a Campden tablet will also prevent fruits such as apples and pears from turning brown, which can affect the final flavour. After racking a wine for the first time, add one Campden tablet, especially to sweet wines. This stabilizes the wine and also prevents further fermentation.

WINEMAKING

INITIAL PREPARATION OF THE MUST

Before beginning to prepare the must, make sure that all the utensils you will be using are very clean, by washing with a solution of sodium or potassium metabisulphite (see page 13.)

The next procedure is to extract as much colour and flavour as possible from the basic ingredient chosen for your wine. The method for doing this depends on the ingredient and its nature.

POURING ON BOILING WATER

This is the most usual way to extract flavour and is suitable for most fruits. Place your chosen ingredient in a polythene bucket or dustbin and pour boiling water over it. Stir the mixture well with a large wooden spoon and leave to cool.

When cool, add a pectin-destroying enzyme (see page 27), following the instructions on the packet, and a crushed or dissolved Campden tablet. Cover the bucket with a lid. Leave to steep in a warm place for 3–4 days, stirring the mixture well once or twice a day.

When the time is up, strain the mixture through a nylon sieve and then through a nylon straining bag into a second polythene bucket, ready for fermentation preparation.

STEEPING IN COLD WATER

This is often the method for making wine from flowers – because boiling water can result in the loss of delicate flavours and essences.

Follow the same instructions as when using boiling water, simply using cold instead. Add two crushed or dissolved Campden tablets to sterilize the must.

Leave to steep as before and strain off in the same way into a second bucket, ready to prepare for fermentation.

EXTRACTION BY BOILING

This is the method used for root vegetables, such as carrot, parsnip, potato and beetroot, which are very hard.

Cut the vegetables into pieces and simmer gently in the water until quite soft but not mushy. The boiling must never be too vigorous, as any pectin present may be released and make it more difficult to extract the juices; you are also more likely to produce a wine that is stubbornly cloudy.

When the vegetables are soft, strain the liquid through a nylon sieve and then through a nylon bag, into a second polythene bucket. When the liquor is cool, add a pectin-destroying agent (see page 27) and a crushed or dissolved Campden tablet. Cover the bucket as before and leave to stand in a warm place for 24 hours, before preparing for fermentation.

PREPARING THE MUST FOR FERMENTATION

Once the colour and flavour have been extracted, prepare the must for the addition of the yeast. For the moment, leave it in the polythene bucket where you have steeped the ingredients.

There are a number of procedures to follow:

1. TEST AND CORRECT THE ACIDITY

An experienced winemaker can tell at this stage if the acidity is correct by tasting the must, however, if you are making wine for the first time, follow the recipe closely. Remember: the point of adding orange or lemon juice or citric acid is to increase the acidity.

Wines made from flowers and herbs naturally contain very little acid. Recipes for such wines are usually fairly accurate, but the acid content of any fruit can vary greatly from season to season, so follow the recipes closely and also check the acid content of the must with litmus paper. This is sold in the form of little books; just tear one leaf out and dip it into the must. The colour it becomes will indicate the acidity. Simply compare the colour with the chart on the front cover of the book – a reading within the limits pH 3–4 is acceptable.

If the acidity is too low, stir in 1–2 teaspoons of citric acid crystals (see page 27). In the case of a few fruit wines, such as rhubarb, the natural acid content may be too high. Neutralize this by adding precipitate of chalk (see page 27) at the rate of 7–15g/¼–½oz to 4.5 litres/1 gallon/ 4¾ quarts liquor. Again, the litmus paper will be useful for checking the result.

2. ADD THE SUGAR

Many old recipes suggest using far too much sugar, which results in a disappointing, syrupy concoction. A finished wine that is too sweet cannot be made dry, but a dry wine can always be made sweeter at the end, by adding more sugar. It is better to add the sugar in stages and to take a hydrometer reading after each addition, so that the initial reading can be near to what is desired.

Add the sugar in the form of a sugar syrup. (Bring 600ml/20fl oz water to the boil, add the sugar and stir until dissolved.) Measure the gravity with the hydrometer (see page 15) as you add the sugar. If you are making a dry wine, the initial hydrometer reading should not exceed 100. Otherwise, some sugar may be left unused after the fermentation process has been completed, and this will leave the wine sweet. It isn't possible to say how much sugar will be needed to reach this point, because of the natural sugars present in the raw ingredient, but it will probably be about 1¼kg/2¾lb. For a sweeter wine, the reading may be in the region of 120.

Whatever the hydrometer reading, record it on a label and tie it around the handle of the bucket, so that subsequent hydrometer readings can be added.

3. ADD THE TANNIN

Tannin may or may not be necessary, according to the nature of the basic ingredient. Again, experienced winemakers can tell by tasting the must. Wines, especially reds, do generally benefit from the addition of a little wine tannin. Add at the rate recommended by the manufacturer. See page 27.

4. ADD THE YEAST AND YEAST NUTRIENT

Many general wine yeasts are available and are simple to use. Stir the appropriate amount of yeast and yeast nutrient thoroughly into the must with a large wooden spoon. See page 27.

5. LEAVE TO FERMENT

Cover the bucket with a lid. Place the bucket in a warm place where a temperature of 15–24°C (59–75°F) can be maintained; the kitchen or an airing cupboard is ideal.

FERMENTATION OF THE MUST

This is the process in which the sugar in the must is converted to alcohol and carbon dioxide by the presence of enzymes secreted in the yeast cells.

1. THE FIRST STAGE

The fermentation may be quite violent at first, so keep the must in the bucket for 4–5 days. Once this stage is over and the fermentation is continuing more slowly, the must is ready to transfer to a fermenting jar or demi-john. Using sterilized equipment, pour the must through a nylon straining bag into another bucket. Check the sugar content using the hydrometer. Record the new reading on the label attached to the bucket handle. (It should be 20–30 points below the initial reading.)

2. THE SECOND STAGE

This takes place in a fermentation jar or demi-john (see page 19). Pour through a sterilized plastic funnel into the jar, filling it only to its shoulder, to allow room for further activity within the jar.

Take a plastic or glass airlock (see page 20) and pour in sodium or potassium metabisulphite solution (see page 13) to a height of about 1cm (½in). Push this through the hole of a rubber bung (see page 20) and fit it tightly into the neck of the demi-john. Attach the label that was around the handle to the handle of the demi-john.

Pour any leftover must into a sterilized bottle and fit with a plug of unmedicated cotton wool. Return both the demi-john and the bottle to the warm place, for fermentation to continue. This second stage of fermentation takes place in the absence of air – an ideal condition for producing alcohol. It continues for several weeks.

Use your hydrometer regularly to check on the progress of fermentation, to tell when the wine is finished and, above all, to find out how much sugar is left once fermentation is complete. If the figure is too low, the wine may be too dry; too high, and it is probably far too sweet.

MATURATION OF THE WINE

This is the term used to describe the ageing of the wine to the point at which it is most pleasant to drink. As soon as fermentation has finished, shake the demi-john and move it to a cooler place. The dead yeast cells, fruit pulp and other solid materials (known as 'lees') will slowly fall to the bottom of the jar, and the wine will start to clear from the top downwards. After a few days and not more than a week, take the clear must, or wine, off the sediment, or the latter will taint the wine with an unpleasant flavour. This process is known as racking (see page 18).

RACKING THE MUST

Racking should be done at frequent intervals, normally about every 4 weeks. Use a siphon, which allows the clearer part of the must to be removed without too much disturbance of the thick, unwanted deposit or 'lees'.

Follow the instructions on page 18. Once you have filled the new demi-john, take a reading with the hydrometer and record it. Add one crushed or dissolved Campden tablet to the wine at the *first racking only*. This inhibits the growth of bacteria and mould, improves the flavour and stabilizes the wine by preventing further fermentation.

- -

WHAT TO DO IF FERMENTATION IS 'STUCK'

Occasionally fermentation begins and then comes to a halt, or gets 'stuck'. There can be a number of reasons for this:

Wrong temperature

The must has become too hot or too cold. The cure is to move the demi-john to a cooler or warmer place, and fermentation should start up again.

Insufficient yeast nutrient

The yeast has died or become inhibited. The cure is to add extra nutrient and some fresh yeast.

Not enough acid

The yeast has died or become inhibited. Test with litmus paper and, if necessary, add more citric acid, and some fresh yeast and yeast nutrient. Stir it well, and it may start up again.

Too much alcohol has formed

The alcohol tolerance of the yeast has been reached and the yeast is inhibited. There is no cure, but this situation can be prevented by the wise use of the hydrometer as already indicated.

Clogged airlock

The must becomes so full of carbon dioxide that the yeast is inhibited. The cure is to pour the wine into a clean jar, allowing it to become aerated.

- -

If you have some of the must reserved in a bottle, use this to fill up the new demi-john to the base of its neck. If you didn't reserve any, fill with water that has been boiled and allowed to cool.

Finally, cork the demi-john tightly and put it away in a cool, dark place, such as a cupboard. Daylight can cause fading of colour, especially with red wines, and deterioration of flavour. Alternatively, cover the demi-john with thick brown paper or a thick brown paper bag, or some dark cloth.

Inspect your wine from time to time, especially if it was still cloudy when put away. As soon as you can see any appreciable deposit – or no more than 8 weeks after putting it away – rack the wine again into a clean demi-john, topping up with cold, boiled water. Store for a further 2 months if it is still cloudy, then rack again. If it is clear, leave it for 4 months before racking.

BOTTLING AND STORAGE

After the wine has been maturing for 9 months or longer, and provided it is brilliantly clear, it may be racked into sterilized bottles.

Taste the wine in the demi-john and add sugar syrup if it is too dry. Siphon into the bottles set out on a tray, or on a thick layer of newspaper.

Let the wine flow down the sides of the bottle rather than splashing into the centre: splashing the wine will lessen its bouquet and increase oxidation. Fill each bottle to about 2cm/¾in above its shoulder so that, once the cork is in place, there is a gap of no more than 2cm/¾in between the bottom of the cork and the top of the wine.

Allow the bottles to stand for a few minutes so that any bubbles of carbon dioxide can escape. When the wine is quite still, insert the corks.

Shake off the surplus moisture from the soaked corks (see page 21), then insert the cork into a corking tool. Put it on the top of the bottle and hit the plunger with a mallet. The cork will slide easily into the neck of the bottle. Dry off the top of the cork with a cloth, then cover with a shrink capsule (see page 21) to seal the cork.

The bottles are now ready for labelling. Record the essential features of the wine: whether sweet or dry; the date it was started; and the alcoholic strength in percentage or proof spirit.

The wine should now be stored in a cool place. The bottles are best kept in a rack that holds them in a slanting position, so that the cork is kept wet by the wine. This prevents the cork from shrinking and excludes the air completely.

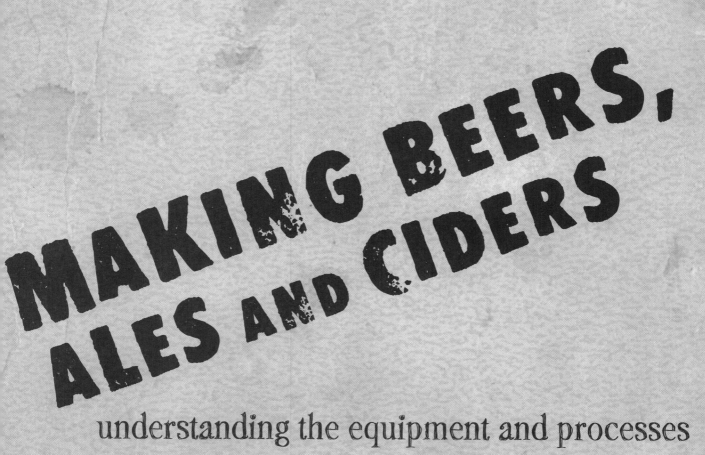

MAKING BEERS, ALES AND CIDERS

understanding the equipment and processes

THE ROOTS OF BEER

Beer and bread are arguably the two culinary foundations of Western civilization. They hold a place in history as the twin strands in the development of food production. Indeed, it is impossible to say which came first: it is difficult for historians to distinguish the process of making bread from the process of making beer. There is evidence that beer recipes were passed from one person to another in the form of a song in ancient Sumer – the region of Mesopotamia between the River Tigris and the River Euphrates, which included the city of Ur and is now part of modern Iraq. Some beers have been brewed from these recipes, but the absence of hops and the addition of dates and other dried fruits means that the modern drink has drifted significantly from its origins in the ancient civilizations. Nonetheless, it clearly has a direct relationship with the drink we know today, and the basic principles for making it remain the same.

Beer contains three main ingredients: water, malted grain and hops. The addition of yeast gives us the drink we know today. Despite its seeming simplicity, the variety of beers that can be created from these four simple ingredients is astonishing: from light, crisp lagers to heavy and dark stouts, cloudy, fruity wheat beers and malty milds. The different blending of the many types of malted barley or wheat with the vast variety of hops available can create beers for every palate.

There are many places one could name as great beer towns and cities of the world. Whether you think it's Pilsen, London, Burton-on-Trent, Dortmund or somewhere else, the great beer styles of the world have grown up around numerous geographic locations then gone on to shift significantly in taste and style through technological change, fashion and commercial pressures. Despite this shifting landscape, the basic principles remain the same and a good pint of beer is made by a process that would still be recognizable to our ancestors.

Making beer is a hobby to enjoy. Many people start with a kit (as I did at first, making some barely drinkable brews), and progress from kits to extract or partial-mash, and then on to full-mash brewing.

EQUIPMENT FOR BEER-MAKING

EQUIPMENT	KIT	EXTRACT	FULL MASH
Hot Liquor Tank	Not Required	Not Required	Optional
Mash Tun	Not Required	Not Required	Required
Boiler	Not Required	Required	Required
Cooler	Not Required	Optional	Optional
Fermenter	Required	Required	Required
Brewer's Paddle	Required	Required	Required
Syphon	Required	Required	Required
Keg/Bottles	Required	Required	Required

The equipment needed for the different types of brewing varies. The progression from kit brewing to full-mash brewing inevitably entails an increase in the variety of equipment required. The equipment for kit brewing can be stored quite easily out of the way; when you make the progression to full mash, the equipment starts to take over somewhat. One of the basic requirements for this hobby is enough room to store all of the kit.

This equipment is specific to brewing beer. Some equipment, such as fermenters and siphons, has already been discussed in The Basics (pages 10–21). This chapter goes into detail only about the equipment that is specific to brewing beer.

MASH TUNS

The mash is the part of the beer-making process when the sugars held inside the malted and crushed grains are converted into a readily available form. This requires the grains to be moistened and held at a reasonably hot temperature over a fairly long period of time.

Many different containers, or 'tuns', can be used. The main requirements are good heat retention and the ability to fill the container with water and then drain it out easily. (Running the water through is not strictly part of the mash, but the two processes are done in the same container.)

Most commercial mash tuns can be replicated at home for less money, so a DIY approach makes a lot of sense.

DESIGNING A MASH TUN

There are two main designs for mash tuns. The first is to take a coolbox and add a drainage system to the bottom of it to allow the wort to drain from the tun. This has the advantage that the coolbox already fulfils one of our two criteria – retaining heat – but draining out the wort may be difficult. The drainage system generally uses a matrix of copper pipe with a large number of slits cut into the underside of the pipe, thus allowing water out while keeping the grain in. There are a number of this type of mash tun available, and good instructions on how to build them online. I recommend a 25–30 litre/5½–6½ gallon/6½–10 US gallon cool box as available in your price range; I am currently using a 24 litre/5 gallon/6½ US gallon coolbox and wish I'd bought a slightly larger one.

The other design uses two fermenters, one with a grid of holes drilled into the bottom and the other with a tap and drainage system installed. The grain is first poured into the top bin and mashed. Then the grains are washed through, and the resulting wort passes through the holes. Alternatively, you can use a plastic dinner plate in a fermenter, with a grid of holes drilled into it. These have the advantage that they promote consistent drainage, but are not as well insulated. That said, adding insulation is not difficult: camping mats and duvets can be pressed into service. There are some good illustrated, step-by-step instructions for these designs online.

Once the grains have been mashed, the process of washing the sugar out can be started. If you are batch sparging (see page 54), no additional equipment is required – although a 2.3 litre/½ gallon/¾ US gallon plastic jug is useful. If you intend to use the fly sparging method, you will need some way of ensuring that the liquor is added to the mash evenly. There are a number of ways this can be done: either put a sheet of tin foil with holes all over it on top of the mash, or use a watering can rose. Some brewers make rotating arms that imitate those used by commercial breweries. The pressure of the water makes the arm rotate, and this motion makes the water run a different way through the mash each time.

BOILERS

A major part of brewing beer, either full-mash or extract brewing, is heating large volumes of water. There is no need to heat water in the same volume if making beer from a kit, so if you only ever intend to brew from kits, you can ignore this section completely.

The fundamental choice to be made when choosing a boiler is either to buy an off-the-shelf pre-made boiler or to make one yourself. There are advantages to both approaches, such as difference in price and amount of time and effort required.

CHOOSING A BOILER

The home-made route is popular with many home brewers; designs and instructions for making a boiler crop up regularly on many home brewing internet forums. The basic design involves a large volume container – 30 litres/6½ gallons/10 US gallons or more – made from food-grade plastic that can withstand the temperatures involved in boiling the wort over a long period of time. I have seen boilers made from large volume fermenters or even beer kegs. These use heating elements taken from domestic kettles to heat and boil the wort. Note, however, that removing the element from a kettle involves potentially unsafe practices, including the removal of shut-off switches. If you make this choice, the responsibility lies with you. For safety reasons, it is obviously a good idea to run a series of test boils prior to using it with wort.

SAFETY

If you are concerned about the safety of a home-made system, there are a number of electric boilers commercially available. These have been rigorously tested and comply with safety legislation. They are, of course, more expensive, and are not without their problems. Most commercial boilers come with an inbuilt simmerstat or thermostatic cutout, and this is not ideal: when boiling wort, there is no setting required other than full, and the wort must be vigorously boiled for the whole time.

There is another option, which does not use electric heaters and so bypasses the safety issues around electricity and boiling liquid. The use of gas to heat and boil in the brewing process is slightly more expensive, but can be very effective. Instead of a large plastic container, a large stainless-steel stockpot is used. These are not cheap, though. The size of the gas burner you will need is a lot bigger than your average camping stove, and a trip to a catering supplier is probably needed. Sizes for burners of this type are typically rated in kW, or BTU in the United States. A brew of the size described in this book requires a burner of 7.5 kW (around 27000 BTU).

It must be stressed that good planning and organization are of paramount importance when brewing. All of the processes should be organized so that you are not required at any point to lift container with a large volume of very hot liquid. It is a much better idea to use a tap or siphon; better still is not to move it at all.

COOLING EQUIPMENT

After boiling, the wort will need cooling, to reach the right temperature for pitching the yeast. The simplest way to cool a brew is to leave it overnight, perhaps in a bath of cold water or ice. If time is an issue, though, you do have other options.

IMMERSION COOLER

This is the simplest and easiest to keep clean. It is a coil of copper pipe, which is placed in the hot wort. Cold water is then pumped through it, picking up the heat. It is easy to make from micro-bore copper pipe shaped around a suitable former. All the connections to the tap and cooler must be very well tightened to ensure that you don't spray your brew room (kitchen in my case) with water when you are cooling – a test run is imperative.

COUNTERFLOW CHILLER

This is more efficient, but not as easy to make or keep clean. Microbore copper pipe is threaded through the middle of some hose. Custom connections at each end allow you to run cold water through the outer hose in the opposite direction, removing the heat and cooling the wort. These work faster, but are more complex to make, and requires more thorough cleaning and sanitization.

PLATE COOLER

This is smaller; most brewers will buy it rather than make it themselves. The wort is passed through the cooler and the fins on it allow heat to escape very quickly. It is small and very efficient, but must be thoroughly clean and sanitized.

STORAGE EQUIPMENT

In no other part of home brewing is the choice of storage vessel so important. For wine, spirits and cider, this is much less crucial. For beer, it comes down to two main choices – to bottle or to keg.

BOTTLING

Bottling has many advantages: you can move bottles around; you can drink a variety of beers rather than being limited to just a few; and the carbonation is generally more reliable than a keg. Kegging has many supporters: it is the traditional way to dispense beer; the flavour profiles develop differently; and the beer is more likely to form a head in the pouring. My preference is to bottle. I like being able to move my beer around, and to have a variety of brews on the go at once. Many brewers swear by kegging systems, though.

THE BASIC KEG AND THE KING KEG

The two simpler types of keg: the budget keg and the king keg use CO_2 generated from secondary fermentation to carbonate the beer. The process takes some time, and is to a certain extent difficult to judge, as to test it is to allow it to lose some of the CO_2 built up. To avoid problems, ensure that the primary fermentation has finished before putting the brew in the keg. This should prevent an excessive amount of CO_2 being created, which can cause the keg to split. This natural fermentation will mean that a sediment is left in the bottom of the keg, which can make moving the keg problematic.

Kegs are easy to use, but do pay attention to the seals on the lid and the tap, to make sure that pressure is held. The threads must be smeared with petroleum jelly to stop gas escaping. A common problem are seals that have been over-tightened, causing them to distort and leak CO_2. The kegs can be used again and again, though the seals will need replacing every so often. It is possible to force CO_2 in through a special lid, to push the last few pints out and keep the beer carbonated, but this should not be necessary if the keg has been properly primed.

The differences between the two are that the king keg has a more pub-style tap, where as the budget keg has a simpler tap and general build quality (although the build quality of the budget kegs is very good).

CORNY KEG

This is a keg with a volume of 19 litres/4 gallons/5 US gallons and fittings for CO_2 at the top, and can be run from smaller or larger CO_2 bottles depending on your preference. It dispenses from the very bottom of the keg, using forced carbonation, not natural carbonation. To stop the sediment from being pushed up, any drinks going into a corny keg must be allowed to drop totally clear in a secondary fermentation vessel before kegging. Corny kegs are the simplest way to install pub-style draught beer taps into your home.

INGREDIENTS FOR BEER-MAKING

There are four main ingredients in any beer: **malted barley**, **hops**, **water** and **yeast**. This section describes each in detail, noting the differences in the various types and how they are used.

BASE MALTS

These provide the basic canvas on which the remaining three ingredients are then placed. Malting is the process of taking the grain, adding water and heat to make it start to germinate, and then stopping the growth completely. This makes the sugars easy to extract. Up to 100% of a grain bill (see Glossary) can be made up from these malts. All malted grains used in brewing need to be crushed in order to be used. They can be purchased uncrushed, but it is easier for the home brewer to buy them already crushed.

PALE MALT

This is the malt used in British-style ales and bitters; the US equivalent is called two-row barley. The colour is between 5.8EBC and 6.8EBC (see Glossary), although extra-pale versions are available.

LAGER MALT

This malt is used in European styles of lager. It is a slightly lighter colour than pale malt at 2.5EBC and 3.8EBC. The flavour can have a biscuit or nut element. There are numerous, generally regional variations, including Vienna malt and Munich malt, which can vary widely in terms of the colour and flavour.

WHEAT MALT

The malting process applied to wheat is an essential part of a wheat beer style. The malt can be used in smaller amounts in other styles as the additional proteins in the wheat aid head retention and give the beer a fuller feel: 3.8–4.8EBC.

MALT EXTRACTS

All of the above malt types are available as malt extract – the sugar elements with some or all of the moisture removed. The are two distinct types: liquid malt extract (LME) and dry malt extract (DME, or Spraymalt). If using in amounts smaller than a whole packet, it is easier to use DME, as storing or measuring LME is difficult. DME tends to have a longer shelf life, and not to alter in colour or flavour over time, but LME, if well kept, can give a better-flavoured beer.

SPECIALITY MALTS

CRYSTAL MALT

This is a classic British speciality malt, used to add a distinct nutty taste, and more body to the beer. It can vary in colour from pale to dark, but the standard, or medium, crystal tends to be 150–160EBC.

SMOKED MALT

This is a speciality type of malt that originates from Bamberg in Germany. It is traditionally smoked with beech. Heavily smoked malts may not be suitable as a base malt, although a traditional Rauchbier can be made with 100% smoked malt. There is a Scottish version that is smoked over peat; it has a more potent smoky flavour and is easy to overuse. 4.6–6.0EBC.

COLOURING MALTS

There are a number of malts that are similar to the base malts but which have been kilned for much longer, giving them a darker colour and more distinct properties. These are not used for large proportions of the brew, and tend to be used for adding colour and character. They include amber malt, 60–100EBC; brown malt; 130–150EBC; chocolate malt, 500–1350EBC; and black malt, 1400–1600EBC.

UNMALTED GRAINS

Not all fermentable sugars come from malted grains; some unmalted grains are used. These require mashing, generally for 90 minutes, before we can extract the elements we want.

ROAST BARLEY

This gives stout its classic grainy coffee flavour and ruby blackness. It tends to be used sparingly. 1600–1700EBC.

FLAKED OR TORRIFIED WHEAT

This is the whole kernel of the wheat which has been heated very quickly and milled to make the sugars more accessible. Where the wheat has not been heated is known as flaked wheat. Flaked wheat is used in larger additions in wheat beer, where it lends the characteristic protein haze of that style. Torrified wheat is used in British styles of beer for head retention and body. 4.0–4.5EBC.

FLAKED OR TORRIFIED MAIZE

This is commonly found in British ales and is used to lighten the colour of the brew without altering the taste too much. 2.0–2.4EBC.

SUGARS AND HONEY

As well as relying on fermentable sugars from grain, some styles call for the addition of sugars from other sources, such as household sugar or sucrose. This is used in small amounts because large volumes can cause the beer to develop a dry cidery finish.

Brewer's sugar is a slightly different sugar, glucose, but is used in the same way as household sugar. Honey can also be used to provide additional fermentable sugars, but if the bulk of the sugars are coming from honey the drink ceases to be a beer and is called braggot. In some of the higher-gravity Belgian styles, sugar is added in the form of Candi Sugar. This comes in a variety of colours and can alter the colour as well as the alcohol content of the finished beer.

HOPS

Hops are an essential element in any beer, for they act as a counterbalance to the sweet flavours of the residual sugars. Without hops, beer would be excessively sweet. Although we think of hops as being the essential choice for this role, they have been widely used only since around the thirteenth century – not very long, given the long history of beer. They are not the only agent used to counteract sweetness. Other herbs and spices have been widely used: heather in Scotland, dates in Mesopotamia. Before the dominance of hops, people used whatever was widely available.

There are three qualities that hops bring to a beer: bitterness, and, for some styles, flavour and aroma.

The bitterness in hop additions comes through the amount of Alpha Acid (or AA) present in the hop; the measurement is given as a percentage. Different hops have different amounts of this acid; more acid means that more bitterness is added to the brew. The hops need to be boiled for a fairly long time to impart the bitterness to the beer. The first hops added to the boil, generally right at the start, are called the bittering hops.

Flavour and aroma come from hops added later in the brew; this is where their individual characteristics will shine through. To a certain extent, the flavours and aromas of hops used early in the boil get lost in the vigour of the boil. Flavouring hops are added in the last half of the boil, and aroma towards the end, or after the boil.

VARIATION AND VARIETY
Hops are a plant whose characteristics change dramatically, depending on their growing conditions – the soil, the growing period and the amount of sun (less or more). A good example is the Styrian Golding hop. A descendant of the British Fuggle, it is grown in the Styria region on the Slovenian/Austrian border. It shares characteristics with the fuggle, but is unique.

There are many hop types, ranging from those high in alpha acids used principally for bittering, to hops that add big flavours and aromas as diverse as grassy to spicy, soft fruits to citrus. These are not the only way to deliver diversity and interest in a beer, but are a contributing factor to many styles. Some hops will deliver on both counts, having enough alpha acids to deliver the bitterness, and enough essential oils to give flavour and aroma. These are known as dual-purpose hops.

CALCULATING ALPHA ACID (AA)
Most hops will have the AA% printed on the packaging. Where this differs from the value for a given recipe, you will need to recalculate.

Software is available, but you can also use the formula below:

$$\text{Substituted Hop Weight} = \frac{\text{Weight of Hops in Recipe} \times \text{AA\% of Hops in Recipe}}{\text{AA\% of Substituted Hops}}$$

This formula also works well if you cannot find a hop suggested for a recipe. Some hops are regionally specific and can be difficult to get outside that region. I live in the United Kingdom, and so rely on hops that are easily available here. If you can't find them, the recipes will still be as good, if a little different, with different hop varieties. For suggested substitutes, see page 48.

Hops should be carefully stored, to preserve the acids and essential oils important in adding flavour to your brew. Ideally they should be kept as cold as possible, with as little oxygen as possible. A good place to keep them is in the freezer.

WATER
Water makes up most of the finished product and so is fundamental in making beer. Most tap water is broadly suitable for brewing beer. However, the famous brewing towns and cities (including London, Pilsen and Burton-on-Trent) have very favourable water profiles. Kit brewing does not require any special treatment for the water, and even extract brewing does not really need much in terms of treatment.

Despite its importance in the process, it can be easy to overlook the quality of your water, and the difference that the right kind of water can make to the quality of the beer. Do nothing in terms of water treatment in the first instance, and see where it gets you. If your gravity is low, or there are some odd flavours, the water can sometimes be the problem (see page 16).

WATER TREATMENT

The subject of water, and water treatment in particular, can quickly degenerate into a chemistry discussion. I've tried to write an understandable water treatment process that anyone can follow – and have glossed over the science bits.

There are two parts to the simple treatment process. The first, and most important, is to boil the water before using it. Boil it for 15–20 minutes on full; prepare an extra couple of litres above your total volume to allow for evaporation in the boil. This should then be run off from the boiling vessel and the boiler cleaned out. This forces out of suspension chemicals that we don't want in the water; they will change the mash pH from the range we want (around pH 5.3) to something higher. This is the simplest step, and has the biggest impact. If you wish to take further steps, add 0.4g/0.06oz of gypsum per litre/1¾ pint/¼ US gallon of water, or 15g/0.5oz for the 37 litres/8⅛ gallons/9¾ US gallons that will be needed for a 23 litre/5 gallon/6 US gallon brew length.

If you find this is not sufficient, there are many books that describe the process of water treatment in fine detail. You could also fine-tune the pH of your mash to the profile of your water

HOP TYPE	AA%	TYPE	SUBSTITUTE HOP
UK Admiral	14.5	Bittering	Target
US Columbus	15.5	Bittering	Centennial, Pacific Gem
UK Target	10.5	Bittering	Admiral
DE Hallertauer Magnum	11.0	Bittering	Galena
NZ Pacific Gem	14.0	Dual Purpose	Columbus, Nugget
NZ Nelson Sauvin	12.5	Dual Purpose	–
US Chinook	10.5	Dual Purpose	Nugget, Eroica, Northern Brewer
UK First Gold	9.0	Dual Purpose	Northern Brewer, Crystal, Galena
UK Northdown	8.0	Dual Purpose	Challenger, Perle, Northern Brewer
UK Challenger	7.0	Dual Purpose	Northern Brewer, Perle
UK Northern Brewer	8.0	Dual Purpose	Northdown, Perle
NZ Willamette	7.0	Dual Purpose	US Willamette, Fuggle
UK Bramling Cross	6.0	Dual Purpose	EK Goldings
UK Progress	5.5	Aroma	Fuggle, First Gold, Progress
DE Tettnang	4.5	Aroma	Hallertauer Mittlefruh, Fuggle, Liberty
UK East Kent Golding	4.6	Aroma	Fuggle, Willamette
SI Styrian Goldings	4.5	Aroma	Fuggle, Willamette
UK Fuggle	4.5	Aroma	Styrian Goldings, Willamette, Tettnang
CZ Saaz	3.0	Aroma	
DE Hallertauer Mittlefruh	5.0	Aroma	Hersbruck, Crystal, Mt Hood

and the requirements of your brew. This can be a lengthy and drawn-out process with many variables, and as such is not described here.

YEAST

Yeast is the essential but often unappreciated ingredient in beer. It is the basis for all of the chemical processes that ensure the beer we drink is more than sweet water.

VARIETIES OF YEAST AVAILABLE

The variety of yeasts is almost as bewildering as the variety in all the other ingredients. It is worth experimenting: even a kit brewer can substitute the standard yeast to see what it achieves. The main differences between yeasts are defined by the temperatures required for fermentation. Lagers require much lower temperatures (9–14°C/48–57°F), while yeasts for ale have a fermentation range much closer to room temperature (15–24°C/59–75°F). It is important to check the individual yeast strain: most manufacturers publish the correct temperature on their website. In some cases, different temperatures provide different flavour profiles in the finished beer. In most cases, fermentation at above the recommended temperature will cause an 'off' flavour similar to nail varnish remover.

STORAGE

Storing yeast for a long period of time is not recommended. It is a living organism and can die. A refrigerator is usually required.

The easiest type of yeast to use is dried yeast. This is sold in 11.5g/0.4oz packets, enough for a brew of 23 litres/5 gallons/6 US gallons, although stronger beers might require more. Packet yeast should be left at room temperature for a couple of days before use, in order to acclimatize, and should be rehydrated at least 30 minutes prior to pitch. To rehydrate your yeast, add it to about 110ml/4fl oz/½ cup of boiled and cooled water, brought down to the optimum temperature for the yeast; this should all be done in sanitised containers.

Also easy to use is a packet with sufficient yeast kept in suspension with a nutrient to start it working before adding it to the wort. This is a relatively new addition to the market. Most liquid yeasts are available as slants. These are test tubes with something for the yeast to live on, containing a smaller number of yeast cells. Yeast slants require the yeast to be grown into a colony big enough to pitch into the wort. This is done by adding a starter (see page 51).

MAKING A YEAST STARTER

A yeast starter should be made 4–5 days before your brew day. All equipment should be sanitized before starting the process.

Equipment:
Glass bottle (approximately 500ml/1 pint)
Airlock
Funnel
Bung suitable for your bottle
Enough tin foil to make a loose cap for the bottle

Ingredients:
300ml/10fl oz/1¼ cups water
60g/2oz Dried Malt Extract (DME)
Yeast slant

Start by boiling the water. Add DME, which should be properly dissolved, and then simmer for 10 minutes. Leave to cool to a reasonable temperature (60°C/140°F), then transfer it to your bottle, and then place it in cold water. The bottle can be shaken to cool it quicker, and add oxygen to the mixture. The cap should be placed on the bottle to stop anything getting in.

Once the mixture has cooled to your yeast's optimum temperature (according to the manufacturer), pitch the yeast and fit the airlock and bung.

The outside of the bottle should be kept clean and dry, and the bottle should be opened and shaken 1–2 times a day to add more oxygen, and promote yeast growth. (There is no need to promote anaerobic growth at this stage; we want high levels of yeast multiplication.)

In order to ensure that you add only the yeast to your brew and not the DME and water used to feed it, put the bottle in the refrigerator and leave overnight. By the next day, when you are ready to brew, the yeast will have dropped to the bottom, leaving just the liquid. The liquid can be siphoned off and discarded, and the yeasty slurry in the bottom can then be washed out with wort from the fermenter and pitched onto the brew.

WAYS OF MAKING BEER

This section describes the process of making beer. Three processes are explained: the use of kits; extract brewing – for those who want more flexibility, but not the same level of investment; and full-mash brewing, which is broadly the method used by commercial brewers.

BEER KITS

Beer kits have a poor reputation, due mainly to the poor-quality kits made in the past, particularly during the 1970s. Modern kits generally use high-quality ingredients and are capable of producing a fine pint of beer. If you want to try making beer, a kit is the best way to start.

There are two types of kits: one-can and two-can. Two-can kits are invariably the premium version, containing all that is required to make 40 pints of beer/5 gallons/6 US gallons. Note that losses to the yeast cake in the bottom mean that you may not get the full 40 pints/5 gallons/6 US gallons.

To use one-can kits effectively, ignore the instructions to use household sugar, and replace this with either spraymalt (DME) or beer kit enhancer (a mixture of DME and brewer's sugar). The other point to note about kits is that the instructions are not generally accurate about the amount of time required for kit beers to become drinkable. It is possible to be drinking full-mash beers in 2–3 weeks. However, kit beers tend to take longer to condition. The rule of thumb is to leave the beer for 1 week per 10 points of specific gravity, perhaps adding an additional week.

As long as your sanitization is good, and you remember these caveats, kits can make very enjoyable beer.

EXTRACT BREWING

This process lies somewhere between making kit beers and full-mash brewing, and can be really useful as a stepping stone between the two. You don't need to do a mash because, unlike a kit, all the sugars come from unhopped malt extract, either liquid or dried. Brewing in this way will give you a good introduction to the boil, which is a vital part of both extract and full-mash brewing.

The only significant issue with brewing extract beers is the cost of malt extract: the beer ends up significantly more expensive than a full-mash brew (sometimes as much as twice the price). For a full-mash brew, you will have the cost of buying more equipment, of course, but this cost is quickly offset after a few brews.

In extract brewing, the bulk of the sugar in the process comes from the extract. However, there is more to the flavour in beer than the basic malt, so some additional grains are required. The extract recipes in this book require you to replace the base malt or malts with liquid or dry malt. Other grains are added to the process because we need the extra colours and flavours they provide; these are known as the speciality grains.

The only extra equipment we need is a grain bag. Made of mesh or muslin, this enables you to add the grains easily and then remove them; excessive boiling can give a beer a grainy, 'off' taste. Not all grains can be used in this way, so an extract version is not given for some recipes.

FULL-MASH BREWING

The recipes in this book have been formulated to be brewed as full-mash recipes. Though extract and kit brews can produce drinkable beers, only full-mash brewing gives you complete control and the ability to create beers of distinction. There are three processes within the initial stages of full-mash brewing: the mash, the sparge and the boil. Each of these is described with step-by-step instructions. Also explained are the problems you might come up against and how to solve them.

THE MASH

This is a simple but necessary stage of the brew, where the conversion of sugars starts, making them easy for the yeast to consume.

In your boiler – or HLT, if you have one – heat 18 litres/4 gallons/4¾ US gallons of water to 76°C/169°F. Mix, to ensure that all the liquor is heated evenly. The correct amount of mash liquor should then be run into the empty mash tun. Slosh this around to ensure that the mash tun is heated.

To the water, slowly add the full amount of grain, and stir it in with your paddle. Take care to ensure

EXTRACT BREWING PROCESS

In all brewing processes, everything *before* the boil needs to be clean but not sanitized. Everything that comes into contact with the wort *after* the boil needs to be cleaned and sanitized.

Bring 16–18 litres/3½–4 gallons/4¼–4¾ US gallons of water to around 40°C/120°F. At the same time, warm the liquid malt extract to ensure that it will come out of the can easily. Once the water is at the right temperature, take it off the heat and add all the malt extracts. Stir thoroughly. Now top the water volume up to as close to the total pre-boil volume as you can. In this book, this level is assumed to be 32 litres/7 gallons/8½ US gallons for a 23-litre/5-gallon/6-US gallon batch, with the remainder lost to the boil. This may vary with different boiler designs. Add the speciality grains to the boiler in a grain bag and turn the heat back on.

Once the water reaches boiling point, take the grain bag out of the boiler; it has done its job of imparting additional flavours to the brew.

At the start of the boil, add the '90-minute hops'. These are the bittering hops and need to be boiled for 90 minutes in order to reach the level of bitterness in the recipes. Once you get to the appropriate point in the boil, add your other additions – hops, protofloc and so on – until it has been boiled for the full 90 minutes.

The wort now needs cooling in exactly the same way as full-mash beers – as outlined on page 55.

that it is not stirred too much, to avoid waterlogged grain, but make sure that there are no dry pockets and that all the grain is mashed.

The temperature should now be taken. It should read 66°C/150°F. If it is too hot, add small amounts of cold water to lower the temperature; if it is too cold, add small amounts of warm, not boiling, water.

This now needs to be closed up, wrapped up and left for a total of 90 minutes. It is possible to do a shorter mash (and, indeed, hotter or colder mashes for different effects), but 90 minutes is a good starting point and gives good results. The recipes in this book have been formulated for this type of mash.

THE SPARGE

Once the sugars have been converted by the mashing process, they must be washed out of the grains and into the liquor to create our wort. This process is the sparge. The batch sparge is the simplest and easiest method for the home brewer. In a batch sparge, the grains are mashed with the volume of liquor specified in the recipe under 'mash liquor'. Then, once the mash is finished, the tun is topped up until it is full, settled and then drained. The rest of the liquor is then used to wash through the grains by filling the tun in equal batches, settling and then draining. This may well be one or two, maybe more batches, until all the liquor has been used.

Whilst the mash is on, heat all the remaining liquor to 80°C/176°F. Use this to top up the mash and fill the mash tun. This should bring the mash up to 77°C/170°F and halt part of the conversion process, making it easier to rinse out the sugar. Leave for 15–20 minutes to allow the grain to settle and ensure that excessive amounts of sediment are not drawn off. After this time, remove the lid.

The first few pints, or first runnings, should then be drawn off (these will be recirculated). Run the wort into a large jug, then pour it carefully back into the top of the mash tun. Once the wort is running clear, you can run it off into the boiler. At the same time, heat the liquor to 77°C/170°F. Once the wort has completely stopped running from the mash tun, close the tap. Now refill the tun with liquor at 66°C/150°F. If there is not enough space, you will need to do a third batch. Put the lid on and leave for a further 15 minutes to settle.

The first runnings of the second batch should be run into a jug until it clear, then run it all off into the boiler. If there is any of the total liquor left at this point, repeat the process as for the second batch, until it has all gone. This should provide your full volume of wort for the boil. If there is more wort than will fit in your boiler, keep it to one side. Then add small amounts to the boil as it loses volume through evaporation.

THE BOIL

This is where the hops come into play along with the copper finings. Whilst it may seem a good idea to try to prevent evaporation, remember that this is an essential part of the process.

Whilst the second batch is settling and running off, switch on the boiler so that the first batch can be brought up to temperature: this will save time later.

Once all the wort has been collected, turn up the temperature to achieve a full rolling boil. Once it reaches full boil, it needs to stay there for 90 minutes. Add the 90 minute hops right at the start. Just pour them on top of the wort, and the action of the boil will mix them in.

As the boil progresses, you will need to add all of the relevant additions in the order, timing and quantity specified in the recipe. If using an immersion cooler, put this into the boil after 15 minutes to ensure it is sanitized. Use this time to sanitize all the equipment you are going to use after this point.

COOLING

The wort needs to be cooled down to pitching temperature. This can be done in numerous ways (see page 42) and can take around 30 minutes for an immersion chiller, and longer for a water bath. More efficient coolers will take less time. The hot run-off water from the immersion cooler can be used for cleaning the boiler and the mash tun if you are using an immersion cooler.

FERMENTATION

The wort will now have a deficit of oxygen in it. Yeast creates alcohol as a by-product in anaerobic (oxygen-free) conditions, but requires oxygen to multiply. Since we will not be pitching enough yeast to ferment the entire brew, we are relying on the initial stages of the fermentation to promote this, and it needs oxygen.

When running the cooled beer from the boiler to the fermentation vessel, use a sieve between the two vessels, which will add oxygen and collect medium-sized bits of hops that get through the boiler filter.

Further aeration can be achieved by adjusting your brewer's paddle to fit into the chuck of a drill, and spinning it rapidly in your cooled wort.

Now is the time to take your original gravity reading, and make a note of it. This will allow you to monitor the fermentation process.

Once the beer is at its correct temperature, and has been aerated, you can pitch the yeast. The beer will now need to be kept at a constant temperature, close to the yeast's optimum temperature, for as long as the fermentation takes. Fermentation has finished once the gravity remains constant for at least 24 hours.

STORAGE

Once the fermentation is complete, if you are bottling or using a simple keg, you will need to prime this with additional sugar to carbonate the brew. If using a forced carbonation system, such as a corny keg, you can ignore the priming. To prime, first run off 300ml/10fl oz/1¼ cups of beer into a sanitized saucepan and add 80g/2¾ oz/6 tbsp sugar. Heat to ensure that the sugar fully dissolves in the beer, but do not allow it to boil.

If bottling, add the extracted beer with the dissolved sugar to the bottom of a second sanitized fermenter, and run the full fermenter of fermented beer into the second fermenting vessel. This will allow the sugar to be fully mixed with the beer and ensure an even coverage across the whole batch, without introducing oxygen to the beer – which would cause it to spoil. The beer should be transferred from the second vessel to the bottles as soon as possible – less than 24 hours after being put into it. Then cap the bottles.

If kegging, put the beer with sugar dissolved in it in the bottom of the sanitized keg, and transfer the full batch of beer into the keg. Ensure that all the seals are prepared as per the product instructions and that CO_2 is not able to leak.

For a corny keg, or other forced carbonation system, the beer should run into a sanitized secondary fermenter until the beer has dropped completely clear. Once clear, it can be transferred to the keg. This can then be carbonated in the normal way for your system.

Beer in kegs and bottles should be conditioned at room temperature for 1 week per 10 points of starting gravity above 1000. It can be drunk sooner, but will often improve significantly with age. The hop bitterness, particularly, can start out quite harsh and will often mellow with age, without losing its bitter edge.

UNDERSTANDING THE BEER RECIPES

The recipes in this book all follow the method outlined in the previous section. Any deviation is fully explained in the recipe, and usually involves the addition of extra ingredients at different times. **Please note that accuracy is vital for the weights, but less so for liquid volumes.** Each recipe details the following:

1 IN MASH	WEIGHT		
Pale Ale Malt	5.22kg		
Medium Crystal Malt	415g		

2 WATER REQUIRED	VOLUME		
Total Liquor	38 litres/8¼ gallons/10 US gallons		
Mash Liquor	14 litres/3⅛ gallons/3¾ US gallons		

3 IN BOIL	WEIGHT	ALPHA ACID	TIME FROM END
UK Admiral	31g	14.5%	90 minutes
Protofloc	1 tsp		15 minutes
UK First Gold	13g	8%	10 minutes

4 STATISTICS			
Expected OG	1052	Colour (EBC)	22.4
Expected FG	1041	Bitterness (IBU)	56.1
Expected ABV	5%		

5 YEAST RECOMMENDATIONS			
	DCL – S04	WLP – 023	WY – 1028

EXTRACT VERSION

6 Malt Extract Required		**7** Steeped Grains	
Light Liquid Malt Extract	3kg	UK Medium Crystal Malt	415g
Light Dried Malt Extract	700g		

1 IN MASH

All the grain and any other additions used in the mash.

2 WATER REQUIRED

The total water, called liquor, required to be treated plus the amount required for the mash.

3 IN BOIL

These are the additions to the boil, shown in order of usage with amounts and times.

4 STATISTICS

The expected gravities at each stage, the bitterness, colours and final alcohol content by volume.

5 YEAST RECOMMENDATIONS

This details the strain of yeast to use – Fermentis, Wyeast or White Labs. These are listed in shorthand: WLP, white labs Yeast; DCL, Fermentis; WY, Wyeast.

6 MALT EXTRACT REQUIRED

This is the amount of malt extract that should be used to replace the full amount of base malt in the brew. If no extract is shown, the recipe is unsuitable for this style of brewing. The amount of liquid extract shown is in multiples of 1.5kg/3.3lbs because it is the size of most cans. This is because it is difficult to measure smaller amounts of liquid extract. The difference is made up from dried extract which is easier to measure.

7 STEEPED GRAINS

The amount of speciality grains used in the recipe.

CIDER, PERRY AND MEAD

The making of cider and perry is relatively seasonal. You can get apples out of season, but you are much more likely to get them at a good price when they are actively falling out of the trees. In many areas, working together as a group or collective to make cider is a good approach. High volumes can be made more reliably, and the cost of specialist equipment is shared. Joining an established group will mean you learn very quickly. Ask around in your local area for groups. Large groups will probably have connections with or even ownership of an orchard or collection of trees; part of the arrangement will involve the care of these.

If you prefer not to be involved with other people, it is possible to gather enough apples to make cider for yourself. Local allotments are a good place to start: a large allotment may have many windfall apples that would otherwise go into compost. Alternatively, trees in public places, friends and neighbours can be a good source; asking around for apples is easy. Do ask nicely: the promise of some excellent cider at the end makes a good bargaining chip! This may also enable you to return in following years, and ensure a good supply.

The recipes are a guide only: they can be followed to the letter, but it's not important. I find it very satisfying to make what I can from what I get. The mead recipes give you an idea of what has gone before. It's a style that lets your imagination run wild: you can put almost anything in a mead. There are, of course, some general styles, some of which are discussed here. But if you have something to hand – be it fruit, herbs or spices – and you can imagine it working with honey, then give it a go! Lemons, oranges, melons, cinnamon, star anise, soft fruit, apples, pears – you name it, it's worth a try.

EQUIPMENT FOR CIDER-MAKING

Making cider and perry is significantly different to that of beers and country wines. Water is added to both of these to make up the volume, but cider and perry is made exclusively from the juice of the relevant fruit, much like grape wines. This major difference means that you will need a couple of extra pieces of equipment.

SCRATTER OR PULPER

Before the juice can be pressed from the fruit, the whole fruits need to be mashed to a pulp. Use a food processor or a fruit juicer.

Alternatively, buy a 'pulp master'. This is a rotary blade affixed to a drill, which will allow you to pulp a large volume of fruit at once. Spinning blades at high speed must obviously be used with caution, particularly because stones or other solid matter may have got into the fruit.

Another idea is to make your own version of a pulper: a couple of interlocking rollers with bolts or nails in them, which will shred and pulp the fruit as you pass them through the rollers. You will need some kind of feeding device to ensure that you don't take your fingers off — a wooden block is often used.

PRESSING

Once you have pulped your fruit, you will need to press the juice out. This will require some kind of pressing mechanism. You can purchase a small press for a modest amount, but I suggest making your own, larger press, which will make make the process easier.

Use a strong wooden stool with a hole in the middle (the holes will often take the form of a handle), add to the top of this a strong wooden tray with a matching hole to allow the juice to run through — this will be a former to ensure the pressing is contained. The tray should be deep enough to contain a decent amount of pulp; this will of course depend on the size of the stool, but 20cm/8in should be enough. The cheeses of pulp will be wrapped in muslin and stacked on top. If there are a number of them, a cheese top will be required. This is just a strong piece of wood to keep the shape of the cheeses of pulp whilst they are being pressed. The top of the press should be a solid board: an offcut from a kitchen work surface can be used for this construction (and it has a wipe-clean surface). In order to press the top down on to the frame of the press, four G-clamps are used, one in each corner of the press, applied evenly to extract the juice.

INGREDIENTS FOR CIDER-MAKING

Many cider purists will say that a proper, good-quality cider must be made from traditional cider apples, and there is an element of truth in this. However, cider can also be made from a mixture of dessert and cooking apples (with perhaps some crab apples added for additional astringency).

CIDER APPLES

Cider apples are traditionally divided into sweet, bittersweet, sharp and bittersharp varieties, and a mixture of these four is used to create the different flavours and sweetness levels. The sharpness is often related to the acid content of the apples. Many traditional cider apple varieties are unsuitable to eat because of their high tannin content, but they do make an excellent cider.

The trees themselves are readily available, and if you have the space, it can be useful to have your own. There are also pick-your-own orchards that offer cider apples, and orchards that sell via mail order. The problem is that many orchards producing cider apples want to sell in very large quantities!

There are some classic apple varieties which are multi-purpose. That is, they can be eaten, used for cooking or made into cider. These are worth considering if you have to buy large quantities of fruit, or are going to plant some trees. The two stand-out varieties are Tom Putt and Egremont Russet, both of which work well in a blend of apples to create cider. Tom Putt has also been used in single-variety ciders with good results.

In the table opposite, which varieties to use for the taste element required have been noted. It's worth remembering that some of these varieties, notably Dabinett, will make very good single variety cider. Others are only suitable for blending; Tremlett's Bitter is the bitterest variety that can easily be found. You could make a single-variety cider out of it, but I wouldn't recommend doing so; it's much better used to complement to other apples, providing depth of flavour and accentuating the flavours of its companions.

Clearly, not all of these varieties are going to be available in quantities we might be able to use, so it's worth considering which more readily available varieties will work in their place. A general rule of thumb is to replace the sweet element in a recipe with a variety of dessert apples; the sharp/acid apples with cooking apples; and the bitter/astringent apples with crab apples. Crab apples are reasonably easy to obtain because they are frequently grown as an ornamental variety. The apples themselves are very small but have a high tannin content, which helps in the development of complex flavours.

PERRY PEARS

Whilst cider can be made from a mixture of dessert and culinary apples, dessert pears lack the tannins to give the perry any body or depth of flavour. This means that perry made exclusively from dessert pears can be thin and a little bit uninteresting. So find a source for perry pears: large established gardens often oblige.

The classic perry pear variety is the Blakeney Red or Painted Lady, which is a medium-sharp, or slightly acid pear. There are many many others, of course. Popular in the sweet category are Hendre's Huffcap and Barnet; in the acid or sharp category, Gin and Yellow Huffcap; and in the bitter or astringent category, Butt and Barland. It is difficult to insist on specific varieties for making perry at home, and the recipes for cider and perry can be mixed and matched between apples and pears.

It is still possible to make perry from dessert pears, and the recipes in this book assume that at least some of your pears will be of this type, since they are readily available. Much like the Kentish blend of apples for cider-making, you can use pears for the bulk of the recipe, and add an amount of a more tannin-rich fruit to give the flavour more dimensions.

MEAD INGREDIENTS

The main fermentable ingredient for mead is honey. This makes it simple to work with because, at its most basic, any honey will do. Often the complexity of flavour in mead comes not from the honey itself but what goes with it.

Clearly, the more flavour your honey has at the start, the more it will have at the end, but it's an ingredient that is much more easy to get hold of than cider apples or perry pears!

In fact, the process for making mead is very simple, and I'd recommend it to beginners. You shouldn't need much more than you would for a simple wine or beer kit.

SWEET APPLES
Sweet Alford, Le Bret. These are an essential ingredient in any Breton-style cider. They are very similar varieties.

BITTERSWEET APPLES
Yarlington Mill, Dabinett, Tremlett's Bitter. The Dabinett makes up a large proportion of many notable top-quality ciders. Tremlett's Bitter needs significant respect in order for cider to maintain any kind of balance: it is a very bitter apple.

BITTERSHARP APPLES
Kingston Black, Tom Putt. These are an essential ingredient; the Kingston can be used in quite high proportions and works well blended with Yarlington Mill.

SHARP APPLES
Crimson King, Camelot.

MAKING CIDER AND PERRY

Making cider and perry is a very simple process – and making mead even more so.

Here, the process for cider and perry is outlined first. All the steps for making cider are required to make perry; and the steps specific to perry are clearly identified. For both methods, be careful with your sanitization. Neither method involves boiling, so sanitization should be scrupulous throughout the process, and every piece of equipment you use should be clean.

STEP 1
Collect your fruit, and measure out the right balance of apples for your cider. These should be ripe and fresh at this point. It is possible to make cider/perry from long-term stored fruit, but the results tend to be better from the freshest fruit.

STEP 2
If you plan to add an additional yeast strain to ferment the fruit, clean the fruit now. Traditional cider is fermented by the natural yeasts in the skins of the fruit, but this increases the possibility of infection. The fruit now needs to mature for around a week after picking.

STEP 3
After a week standing, all rotten fruit should be discarded. If making a small batch – less than 25 litres/5 gallons/6 US gallons – any small blemishes should be removed. A large volume of juice will ensure that any blemishes in the fruit do not impact on the overall flavour, but problems can be more obvious in a smaller batch.

STEP 4
Once the fruit has matured, it needs to be pulped, to create a loose pulp known as pomace.

Perry only
Perry Pomace must stand overnight in order for the pomace to lose some of the tannins.

STEP 5
The pomace now needs stacking into the press. If you are using an open-style press, you will need to make 'cheeses' of pomace. Wrap the pomace in sheets of muslin or net curtain and put them inside a former the correct size for the press. The cheeses should be around 10–15cm/4–6in thick and stacked on top of each other. If you are pressing one or two cheeses, you won't need to

put anything between the cheeses. More than two, and you will need a 'cheese top' between each cheese. This is just a thick board the same size as the press/cheese; a lattice of wood or a suitably sized chopping board will do, even a plastic one.

STEP 6

Press the fruit. Aim for about 4.5 litres/1 gallon/4¾ quarts of juice from around 10kg/22lbs of fruit. This can vary significantly from variety to variety, and even from year to year; environmental conditions have an impact on how much juice each fruit contains.

STEP 7

If you plan to use a specific yeast strain, add one crushed Campden tablet for every 4.5 litres/1 gallon/4¾ quarts of juice, then leave to stand for 48 hours.

STEP 8

Check the gravity. It should be around 1055 (though it may be significantly higher). If it is lower, you will have a weaker cider or perry, though this is not that much of an issue. If you want it to be stronger, add household caster sugar until it reaches this level, dissolving it first in a small amount of the cold juice. Don't heat the juice to encourage the sugar to dissolve, because this can spoil the flavour. A rule of thumb is that 15g/9½oz/1 tbsp of sugar will raise 4.5 litres/1 gallon/4¾ quarts of liquid by 1 degree of gravity. Generally, a traditional cider or perry will not use any additional sugar.

Perry only
After a particularly hot summer, pears can develop reasonably high concentrations of unfermentable sugars, which will produce a higher final gravity, and a sweeter drink.

STEP 9

Place the juice in a fermenter. If you are using a yeast strain, pitch it first; if you are using natural yeasts, leave the juice to ferment. A good cider strain to use is White Labs 775 English Cider Yeast, or Wyeast 4766 Cider. If you can't find these, a wine yeast can be used for a Breton-style flavour, or an ale yeast for a more traditional flavour. That said, the specific cider yeasts tend to allow the fruit flavours through more effectively.

STEP 10

The fermentation. If you are using a demi-john, this should have a bung and airlock; for a bucket, whatever is required for the design.

STEP 11

The cider should be fermented until no more bubbles are rising and the gravity is stable for three days or more. This should take 10–14 days, or longer in cool weather.

STEP 12

Rack off the cider to another container, preferably one that is identical to the first; a demi-john is ideal. The cider should now be matured in bulk for at least 6 months, if not longer – 8 to 9 months is good. After this time, the cider should be bottled or kegged. If maturing in bulk is not possible, bottle the cider at this point, but be aware that quite a lot of sediment is likely to fall out of suspension in the bottle.

STEP 13

Traditional cider is flat. To carbonate it, you could keg or bottle it with some priming sugar. The cider will eventually have a slight fizz.

MAKING MEAD

Mead is made using water and honey and, in some ways, the process is similar to making beer. For example, if you wish to treat your water, follow the procedures outlined on page 48.

STEP 1
You need as much water as the quantity of mead you intend to make. These recipes assume 4.5 litres/1 gallon/4¾ quarts the size of a standard demi-john.

STEP 2
There are two ways of combining the honey and water: the easy way, suitable for cheap honey, is to heat the water to boiling point, then to let the temperature drop – 75°C/167°F is ideal – and finally to add the honey. The harder way is good for aromatic honey with delicate floral aromas that can be destroyed by heat. Honey is sterile and unlikely to contain yeasts, so heat the water to only 37–40°C/98–104°F and warm the jars of honey in a bath of hot, but not boiling, water. Then tip the honey into the water. Whichever method you use, the honey must be completely dissolved.

STEP 3
Start fermentation. Try Wyeast 4184 or White Labs WLP 720 for sweet mead; Wyeast 4632 for a dryer mead. Most commercial meads are sweet, but dry meads give a different flavour profile. Alternatively, use a generic wine yeast for a dry mead, and a sweet wine yeast for a sweeter mead. Add yeast nutrient for better yeast development, to sustain it through the fermentation.

STEP 4
Fermentation is slow, taking at least 4 weeks. The brew should not be racked during this time.

STEP 5
At the end of the fermentation, rack the mead into a bulk storage container for maturing. Continue racking every 2 weeks (or at least once a month) until there is no sediment, or lees, in the bottom.

STEP 6
The long maturing time means that the mead has a brilliant clarity. If not, use a fining agent.

STEP 7
The maturing process needs at least 3 months, ideally a year. And if you have more time, it tends to improve with age. Once matured, the mead can be bottled and stored. Bottling should not be undertaken early in the process, as mead fermentation is slow and can restart.

PART TWO
THE RECIPES

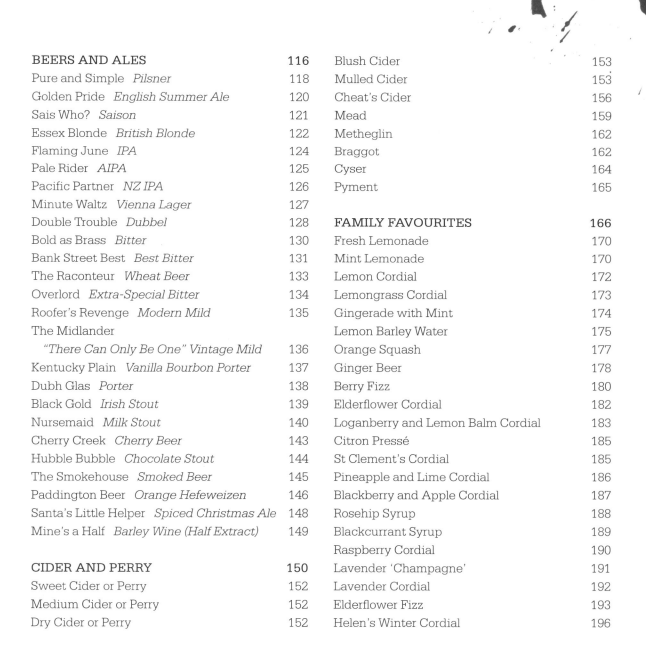

FRUIT WINES AND SPIRITS

oooh fruity!

BLACKBERRY WINE

One of the great country wines. Use only large black fruits that are fully ripe and have been picked on a dry, sunny day, as wet berries never seem to make good wine. Make the berries into wine immediately.

Ingredients

2.75kg/6lb freshly picked, very ripe blackberries

Boiling water (see method)

Pectin-destroying enzyme

Citric acid (if needed)

1.2kg/2½lb/6 cups sugar

Tannin (see pages 31–33)

Yeast and yeast nutrient (see pages 31–33)

Remove any leaves and stalks from the fruit, then place in a polythene bucket. Pour on 3.6 litres/ 6 pints/3¾ quarts boiling water. Allow to become lukewarm, then crush the fruit with a wooden spoon. Add the pectin-destroying enzyme, then cover and leave for 4–5 days, stirring twice daily.

Strain and press the fruit in a fine nylon bag collecting the juice in a clean, polythene bucket. Test the acidity, although it is very unlikely that more acid will be needed and, if necessary, add citric acid.

Dissolve the sugar in 600ml/20fl oz boiling water and add to the clean, polythene bucket. Take a reading with the hydrometer and record it. Finally add the tannin, yeast and yeast nutrient. Cover with a lid, then put in a warm place to ferment. (See pages 31–33 for instructions on how to deal with wine as it ferments and matures, bottling and storage.)

DAMSON WINE

Damsons and bullaces (wild plums) make a rich red wine, which is best kept for at least 6 months after bottling, before opening. Cool the boiling water a little before using, as pectin is very easily released from damsons, and this will lead to cloudy wine.

Ingredients
2.5kg/5lb ripe damsons
Boiling water (see method)
Pectin-destroying enzyme
Citric acid (if needed)
1.2kg/2½lb/6 cups sugar
Tannin (see pages 31–33)
Yeast and yeast nutrient (see pages 31–33)

Remove any stalks from the damsons and wash well. Place in a polythene bucket. Allow 4 litres/7 pints/4¼ quarts boiling water to cool a little, then pour over the fruit. Leave to cool further, then crush the fruit. Add the pectin-destroying enzyme, cover and allow to steep for 3–4 days, stirring twice daily.

Strain and press the fruit through a nylon bag into a clean polythene bucket, then test the acidity, adding citric acid if necessary. Dissolve the sugar in 600ml/20fl oz boiling water and add this to the liquor. Take and record a hydrometer reading and then add the tannin, yeast and yeast nutrient. Leave in a warm place to ferment. (See pages 31–33 for instructions on how to deal with wine as it ferments and matures, bottling and storage.)

CHERRY WINE

Use any colour of cherries, or a mixture, to give a white or red wine. Avoid under-ripe or badly damaged fruit, although split cherries can be used.

Remove any stalks from the fruit and wash and dry. Put in a polythene bucket and pour in 3.6 litres/6 pints/3¾ quarts boiling water. Allow it to cool, then crush the cherries with a large wooden spoon, without smashing the stones. Add the pectin-destroying enzyme, then cover the bucket and leave to steep for 3–4 days, stirring the contents twice daily.

Ingredients

3.75kg/8lb ripe cherries
Boiling water (see method)
Pectin-destroying enzyme
Juice of 1 large lemon
Citric acid (if needed)
1.2kg/2½lb/6 cups sugar
Tannin (see pages 31–33)
Yeast and yeast nutrient (see pages 31–33)

Strain into a clean polythene bucket, using a nylon bag. Add the lemon juice and test the acidity. Add citric acid if necessary. Dissolve the sugar in 600ml/20fl oz boiling water and add to the liquor. Take and record a reading with the hydrometer, then add the tannin, yeast and yeast nutrient. Put in a warm place to ferment. (See pages 31–33 for instructions on dealing with wine as it ferments and matures, bottling and storage.)

MARIGOLD WINE

Use old-fashioned 'pot marigolds', to make this pleasant white wine. Gather the flowers when fully out, on a dry, sunny day, and use only the petals, without any green stalks.

Ingredients

3 litres/6 pints/2¾ quarts freshly picked
marigold flowers
2 medium oranges
2 medium unwaxed lemons
Boiling water (see method)
Citric acid (if needed)
1.2kg/2½lb/6 cups sugar
Tannin (see pages 31–33)
Yeast and yeast nutrient (see pages 31–33)

Place the flower heads in a polythene bucket with the thinly pared rinds of the oranges and lemons. Pour in 4 litres/7 pints/4¼ quarts boiling water, then cover and leave to steep for 3–4 days, stirring twice daily.

Strain off the liquor through a nylon bag into a clean polythene bucket, squeezing out the flowers as much as possible. Add the juices from the oranges and lemons, then test the acidity, correcting with citric acid if necessary.

Dissolve the sugar completely in 600ml/20fl oz boiling water and add to the liquor. Take a reading with the hydrometer, then add the tannin, yeast and the yeast nutrient. Cover with a lid and leave in a warm place to ferment. (See pages 31–33 for instructions on how to deal with wine as it ferments and matures, bottling and storage.)

DANDELION WINE

Bright yellow dandelion flowers bloom profusely and make a fine strong wine. The important thing is to gather the flowers on a sunny day, when they are fully open, and then make the wine immediately.

Ingredients

2.4 litres/4 pints/2¼ quarts fresh dandelion heads or 1 packet dried dandelions

2 medium oranges

2 medium unwaxed lemons

Boiling water (see method)

Citric acid (if needed)

1.2kg/2½lb/6 cups sugar

Tannin (see pages 31–33)

Yeast and yeast nutrient (see pages 31–33)

Press the yellow flower heads lightly into a measuring jug, discarding as much green as possible (without being too fussy about it), to measure out the stated quantity.

Put the flowers in a polythene bucket and add the thinly pared rinds from the oranges and lemons. Pour in 4 litres/7 pints/4¼ quarts boiling water. Press the flowers down with a wooden spoon, then cover and leave to steep in a warm place for 3–4 days, stirring them around thoroughly twice a day.

Strain the liquor through a nylon bag into a clean polythene bucket, squeezing out as much liquid as possible. Add the juice from the oranges and lemons, then check the acidity. Use citric acid to adjust the acidity if necessary.

Dissolve the sugar in the remaining 600ml/20fl oz boiling water and add to the clean polythene bucket. Take a reading with the hydrometer, then add the tannin, yeast and yeast nutrient. Cover with a lid and leave to ferment. (See pages 31–33 for instructions on how to deal with wine as it ferments and matures, bottling and storage.)

ELDERBERRY WINE

Herbalists have long enjoyed using elderberries for making wines and medicinal syrups. A glass of hot elderberry wine taken before bed is a fantastic cold cure.

Ingredients

2kg/4lb freshly picked elderberries
Boiling water (see method)
Pectin-destroying enzyme
1.2kg/2½lb/6 cups sugar
1 medium lemon
Citric acid (if needed)
Yeast and yeast nutrient (see pages 31–33)

Remove the berries from every bit of green stalk by pulling the bunches through the tines of a fork. (The stalks give a bitter taste to the wine.)

Place in a polythene bucket and pour in 3.6 litres/6 pints/3¾ quarts boiling water. When cool, crush the berries with a large wooden spoon and add the pectin-destroying enzyme. Cover with a lid and leave in a warm place for 4 days, stirring it twice a day.

Strain and press the liquor through a nylon bag into a clean polythene bucket. Now add the lemon juice and check the acidity. Add citric acid if necessary.

Dissolve the sugar in 600ml/20fl oz boiling water. Cool, then add gradually to the must, taking a hydrometer reading. Add the yeast and yeast nutrient. Cover again and leave to ferment. Leave elderberry wine for at least a year before opening, preferably three years, as the older it is before drinking the better it tastes. (See pages 31–33 for instructions on how to deal with wine as it ferments and matures, bottling and storage.)

N.B. Sometimes you can end up with an excess of tannin in elderberry wine, caused by using too much fruit, by soaking for too long, or pressing too hard. If a finished wine is a little too harsh, it can often be vastly improved by the addition of a little sugar.

GOOSEBERRY WINE

It is a shame that luscious red dessert gooseberries don't make good wine. But one of the best of all country wines is made from tart green gooseberries, preferably picked just before they begin to colour and soften.

Ingredients

2.75kg/6lb green gooseberries
Boiling water (see method)
Pectin-destroying enzyme
Citric acid (if needed)
1.2kg/2½lb/6 cups sugar
Tannin (see pages 31–33)
Yeast and yeast nutrient
(see pages 31–33)

Top, tail and wash the gooseberries, then place in a polythene bucket. Pour in 4 litres/7 pints/4¼ quarts boiling water, then cover and allow to cool. Crush the berries using a large wooden spoon, then add the pectin-destroying enzyme. Cover again and leave for 2–3 days more, stirring well twice daily. Strain through a nylon bag, pressing the fruit to extract as much liquor as possible, into a clean polythene bucket. Now check the acidity. (If hard, unripe fruit has been used, it is likely that very little extra acid will be needed, but if the berries are soft and ripe, up to 1 rounded teaspoonful citric acid will be necessary.)

Dissolve the sugar completely in 600ml/20fl oz boiling water and cool, then add to the liquor. Take a reading with the hydrometer, then add the tannin, yeast and yeast nutrient. Cover with a lid and leave to ferment. (See pages 31–33 for instructions on how to deal with wine as it ferments and matures, bottling and storage.)

PARSNIP WINE

Parsnips make one of the best of all country wines, but like all root vegetable wines, parsnip takes a year or more to reach its peak. The wine is improved by using parsnips that have endured some heavy frosts, so make it in the winter.

Ingredients
2kg/4lb parsnips
25g/1oz dried root ginger, well bruised (optional)
Water (see method)
175g/6oz/generous 1 cup raisins, washed in hot water and finely chopped
2 medium oranges
2 medium unwaxed lemons
Pectin-destroying enzyme
Citric acid, if needed
1.2kg/2½lb/6 cups sugar
Tannin (see pages 31–33)
Yeast and yeast nutrient (see pages 31–33)

Scrub the parsnips and cut out any brown bits, but don't peel them. Chop into medium-sized pieces – if too small, the pieces will cook to a pulp and your wine will be cloudy.

Simmer the parsnips with the root ginger in 3.6 litres/6 pints/3¾ quarts water, until tender but not mushy. Strain off the hot liquor through a nylon bag and add to the raisins and thinly pared rinds of the oranges and lemons, in a clean polythene bucket. Add 600ml/1 pint/2½ cups cold water and leave to cool. Stir in the pectin-destroying enzyme, then cover and leave for 24 hours.

Add the juices from the oranges and lemons and test the acidity, adding extra citric acid if necessary.

Dissolve the sugar in 600ml/20fl oz boiling water, then stir into the liquor. Take and record a hydrometer reading, then add tannin, yeast and yeast nutrient. Pour into a clean polythene bucket, cover with a lid and leave in a warm place to ferment. (See pages 31–33 for instructions on how to deal with wine as it ferments and matures, bottling and storage.)

PARSLEY WINE

A delightful herb wine that is particularly good as an accompaniment to fish. If you try to grow parsley in your garden or allotment, it either fails miserably or the crop is too bountiful, in which case this a good way to use the excess. Take care not to include any stalks.

Ingredients
450g/1lb fresh parsley leaves
2 medium oranges
2 medium unwaxed lemons
15g/½oz dried root ginger, bruised well
Water (see method)
350g/12oz/2 cups sultanas, washed in hot water and finely chopped
Pectin-destroying enzyme
Citric acid (if needed)
1.2kg/2½lb/6 cups sugar
Tannin (see pages 31–33)
Yeast and yeast nutrient (see pages 31–33)

Wash the parsley, then simmer it very gently with the thinly pared rinds of the oranges and lemons, the bruised ginger and 3.6 litres/6 pints/3¾ quarts cold water, for about 20 minutes. (Make sure that the mixture is always simmering very gently, rather than boiling vigorously, or pectin may be released. This will make it more difficult to extract the juices and is likely to produce a cloudy wine.)

Strain through a nylon sieve into a polythene bucket containing the chopped sultanas and a further 600ml/1 pint/2½ cups cold water. When cool, add the pectin-destroying enzyme, cover and allow to stand for at least 24 hours.

Add the juices from the oranges and lemons. Check the acidity, adding citric acid if necessary.

Dissolve the sugar completely in 600ml/20fl oz boiling water and when cool, stir into the liquor. Take a reading with the hydrometer, then add the tannin, yeast and yeast nutrient. Cover closely and leave to ferment for 1 week.

Strain through a fine nylon bag, pressing the sultanas to extract as much liquid as possible, then continue the fermentation in a clean polythene bucket. Cover with a lid and leave in a warm place to ferment. (See pages 31–33 for instructions on how to deal with wine as it ferments and matures, bottling and storage.)

PEAPOD WINE

A really delicious wine, especially after two years. Use fresh, young, tender peapods, after shelling the peas to eat later.

INGREDIENTS
2.5kg/5lb young peapods
Boiling water (see method)
Pectin-destroying enzyme
2 teaspoons citric acid,
plus extra if needed
1.2kg/2½lb/6 cups sugar
Tannin (see pages 31–33)
Yeast and yeast nutrient (see pages 31–33)

Wash the peapods well, then simmer gently in 4 litres/7 pints/4¼ quarts water, until tender. Strain off the liquor through a nylon bag into a clean polythene bucket, cover and leave to cool. Add the pectin-destroying enzyme, cover again and leave for 24 hours.

Next day, stir in the citric acid and test the acidity; add more citric acid if necessary. Dissolve the sugar in 600ml/20fl oz boiling water and stir into the liquor. Take and record a hydrometer reading, then transfer into a clean polythene bucket. Add the tannin, yeast and yeast nutrient, then leave in a warm place to ferment. (See pages 31–33 for instructions on how to deal with wine as it ferments and matures, bottling and storage.)

APPLE WINE

One of the finest country wines. Use many different varieties of apple for the best flavour, but avoid russets. Cooking apples make better wine than eating apples. If you include up to 10 per cent crab apples, you don't need to add any tannin.

Ingredients

2.75–4.5kg/6–10lb apples
Water (see method)
2 Campden tablets, crushed or dissolved
Pectin-destroying enzyme
1 teaspoon citric acid
1.2kg/2½lb/6 cups sugar
Yeast and yeast nutrient (see pages 31–33)
Tannin, if necessary (see pages 31–33)

Wash the apples, then remove the stalk and flower ends and cut out any brown pieces; don't peel them. Cut into very small pieces and place immediately in a polythene bucket with 3.6 litres /6 pints/3¾ quarts water and the Campden tablets. Add the pectin-destroying enzyme and cover with a lid. Leave for up to 1 week, stirring vigorously with a wooden spoon twice a day.

Strain the liquor from the pulp through a nylon bag, squeezing out as much juice as possible, into a clean polythene bucket. Add citric acid and test the acidity.

Dissolve the sugar in 600ml/20fl oz boiling water, then cool and stir into the must gradually, checking with the hydrometer. Lastly, add the yeast and yeast nutrient; add tannin if necessary. Cover with a lid and leave in a warm place to ferment. (See pages 31–33 for instructions on how to deal with wine as it ferments and matures, bottling and storage.)

PLUM WINE

Different types of plums can be used to make red or white wine. Greengages also make good wine. Pectin is very easily released from all plums, so cool the boiling water a little before pouring it over the fruit, to make sure that your wine will not be cloudy.

INGREDIENTS
2.75kg/6lb ripe plums
Boiling water (see method)
Pectin-destroying enzyme
Citric acid, if needed
1.2kg/2½lb/6 cups sugar
Tannin (see pages 31–33)
Yeast and yeast nutrient (see pages 31–33)

Remove any stalks from the plums, wash the fruit and place it in a polythene bucket. Allow 4 litres/ 7 pints/4¼ quarts boiling water to cool a little before pouring it over the plums. When quite cool, mash the fruit with a wooden spoon and add the pectin-destroying enzyme. Cover the bucket and allow it to stand for 3–4 days, stirring twice daily.

Strain and press the fruit liquor through a nylon bag into a clean polythene bucket. Test the liquor for acidity, and add citric acid if necessary. Dissolve the sugar in 600ml/20fl oz boiling water and add to the bucket. Now take a reading with the hydrometer, ensuring that the sugar quantity will produce the type of wine you want. Add tannin, yeast and yeast nutrient. Cover with a lid, then leave in a warm place to ferment. (See pages 31–33 for instructions on how to deal with wine as it ferments and matures, bottling and storage.)

QUINCE WINE

Use very ripe, mellow quinces, which have turned golden, for wine making. Wash off any grey fluff before grating.

INGREDIENTS

2kg/4lb very ripe quinces
2 Campden tablets, crushed or dissolved
1.2kg/2½lb/6 cups sugar
Boiling water (see method)
2 medium unwaxed lemons
Citric acid (if needed)
Pectin-destroying enzyme
Tannin (see pages 31–33)
Yeast and yeast nutrient (see pages 31–33)

Grate the quinces (as near to the core as possible), into a polythene bucket containing 4 litres/ 7 pints/4¼ quarts cold water and the Campden tablets. Add the thinly pared rind of the lemons and the pectin-destroying enzyme. Cover with a lid and leave in a warm place for up to 1 week, stirring vigorously with a wooden spoon twice daily.

Strain the liquor from the pulp through a nylon bag, squeezing out as much juice as possible into a clean polythene bucket. Add the lemon juice, then test the acidity. Add citric acid if necessary.

Dissolve the sugar in 600ml/20fl oz boiling water, cool, then add gradually to the must, checking with the hydrometer. Finally, stir in the tannin, yeast and yeast nutrient. Cover the bucket again and leave in a warm place to ferment. (See pages 31–33 for instructions on how to deal with wine as it ferments and matures, bottling and storage.)

RHUBARB WINE

The red parts of the stalks of unforced rhubarb are best for making wine. Rhubarb contains an excess of oxalic acid, which is rather unpleasant and is best removed by the use of precipitate of chalk.

INGREDIENTS

2.75kg/6lb freshly picked rhubarb, preferably red
Water (see method)
15g/½oz/1 heaped tbsp precipitate of chalk
1.2kg/2½lb/6 cups sugar
Tannin (see pages 31–33)
Yeast and yeast nutrient (see pages 31–33)

Wipe each stick of rhubarb with a damp cloth and cut it up into short lengths. Put it into a polythene bucket and pour in 4 litres/7 pints/4¼ quarts cold water. Cover the bucket and allow it to steep for 3–4 days. During this time, stir twice daily and break up the fruit as much as possible to release the juice.

Strain off the liquor through a nylon bag and squeeze out as much juice as possible from the fruit into a second polythene bucket.

Mix 7g/¼oz/½ tbsp of the precipitate of chalk to a smooth paste and stir it into the rhubarb liquor. When the foaming has subsided, test the pH with litmus paper. Add the remaining precipitate of chalk, or less, if it seems necessary, to achieve the desired acid level – between pH 3 and pH 4.

Dissolve the sugar in 600ml/20fl oz boiling water, then add to the liquor. Pour into a clean polythene bucket and use the hydrometer to take a reading; remember to record it. Finally add the tannin, yeast and yeast nutrient. Cover with a lid and leave in a warm place to ferment. (See pages 31–33 for instructions on how to deal with wine as it ferments and matures, bottling and storage.)

ELDERFLOWER WINE

Rightly called the queen of the flower wines, this has the most delicate fragrance and flavour imaginable. Pick fresh flower heads in full bloom on a dry, sunny day. Shake gently to dislodge any insects, then snip off the green, fleshy stems because these will make the wine bitter. Press the freshly picked flowers lightly into a measuring jug and use only 600ml/1 pint/generous 1 US pint of blossoms, or the delicate perfume of the wine may suddenly change into 'tomcat'!

Ingredients
600ml/1 pint/generous 1 US pint fresh elderflowers
2 medium oranges
2 medium unwaxed lemons
Boiling water (see method)
Citric acid, if needed
1.2kg/2½lb/6 cups sugar
Tannin (see pages 31–33)
Yeast and yeast nutrient (see pages 31–33)

Place the blossoms in a polythene bucket with the thinly pared rinds from the oranges and lemons. Pour in 4 litres/7 pints/4¼ quarts of boiling water, then press the flowers down with a wooden spoon. Cover and then leave to steep in a warm place for 3–4 days, stirring twice daily.

Strain the liquor through a fine nylon bag into a clean polythene bucket, squeezing out as much of the liquid as possible. Add the juice from the oranges and lemons and test the acidity, adding citric acid if needed.

Dissolve the sugar in the remaining 600ml/20fl oz boiling water, then add to the bucket. Record the reading on the hydrometer, then add the tannin, yeast and yeast nutrient. Cover with a lid and leave to ferment. (See pages 31–33 for instructions on how to deal with wine as it ferments and matures, bottling and storage.)

GORSE WINE

This fragrant gorse wine is one of the best home-made wines. It is made from the golden blossoms only. Pick the flowers on a dry, sunny day and use immediately. Press the flowers down gently into a measuring jug to measure out the stated quantity.

Ingredients

4.5 litres/8 pints/4 quarts fresh gorse flowers

Boiling water (see method)

1.35kg/3lb/6¾ cups sugar

2 medium oranges

2 medium, unwaxed lemons

Citric acid, if needed

Tannin (see pages 31–33)

Yeast and yeast nutrient (see pages 31–33)

Place the gorse flowers in a piece of muslin and tie into a bag with cotton thread. Drop into 4 litres/7 pints/4¼ quarts boiling water, then simmer gently for 15 minutes. Remove the bag, squeeze it well to extract the liquor and add this to the rest of the liquor. Pour into a polythene bucket.

Dissolve the sugar in 600ml/20fl oz boiling water and add to the bucket with the juices and thinly pared rinds of the oranges and lemons. Test the acidity, and correct with citric acid, if necessary. Allow to cool, then add the tannin, yeast and the yeast nutrient.

Cover closely and leave in a warm place to steep for 3 days to extract colour and aroma, stirring twice daily. Strain through a nylon bag into a clean polythene bucket. Cover with a lid and leave to ferment. (See pages 31–33 for instructions on how to deal with wine as it ferments and matures, bottling and storage.)

FRUIT, FLOWER AND HERB LIQUEURS

For centuries fruit-, flower- and herb-flavoured wines and spirits have been made all over the world, both for pleasure and for reasons of health. Known as waters, ratafias or cordials, they are very easy to make at home and are always successful.

Many people make sloe gin, but never think of experimenting with other fruits – strawberry gin and raspberry vodka are just as delightful. All that is required is enough patience to wait while the fruit, flower or herb and the spirit or wine exchange flavours. At the end, you often have the bonus of a delicious marinated fruit to eat as well as the liqueur.

Fresh berries and stone fruits are the best to use. They should be ripe – but not overripe. Herbs, flowers, spices and other seasonings should be as fresh as possible. Always use whole spices, or the liqueur will be cloudy.

The choice of alcohol depends on personal preference – any kind can be used, provided it has an alcoholic content of at least 37.5 per cent by volume. Brandy is the classic spirit for cherries, apricots, raspberries and blackcurrants. The most popular is probably gin, but vodka is tasteless and therefore goes with anything! The only equipment you need is a large preserving jar or lidded jar; a nylon sieve or large funnel, lined with a double layer of muslin; and a screw-capped bottle (the original spirit or wine bottle is ideal).

CASSIS

Cassis is a syrupy blackcurrant drink or flavouring, invented in nineteenth-century France. It is most commonly made with brandy or gin, but vodka can also be used. A small cinnamon stick and a whole clove can be added to the syrup, to give a touch of spice.

Ingredients
450g/1lb/3 cups fresh or frozen blackcurrants
450g/1lb/2¼ cups caster sugar
600ml/1 pint/2½ cups brandy
A few tips of young blackcurrant leaves for extra flavour

Pick over the fruit, discarding leaves and stalks, then wash it. Don't bother to top and tail. Put in a bowl and crush with a wooden spoon, then transfer into a large, sterilized, preserving jar or screw-top jar with the sugar, brandy and blackcurrant leaves.

Leave on a sunny window sill for 1 month, stirring the mixture and turning the jar twice a week. Line a large funnel or nylon sieve with a double layer of muslin and strain the liqueur into a sterilized, screw-capped bottle. Seal and label.

The cassis is now ready to use. Drink as a liqueur; as a long drink with ice and sparkling mineral water; or as a Kir with white wine. Cassis is also a good flavouring for sweet dishes and as a sauce to pour over ice cream and meringues. A tablespoon of cassis added to stews, casseroles and savoury sauces can really lift a dish.

Bilberry Liqueur

Use bilberries instead of blackcurrants and reduce the amount of sugar to 350g/12oz/ 1¾ cups. Mix the liqueur with white wine to make 'Myr' (*myrtille* is French for 'bilberry'), which is popular in parts of France.

CHERRY BRANDY

Cherry brandy is one of the great liqueurs made with brandy – traditionally, brandy in which wild cherries have been steeped. Cultivated Morello cherries are ideal because they are less sweet than other varieties, but you can use any dark, flavoursome cherry. It takes about 6 weeks for fermentation to stop and the sugar to dissolve fully, but it is better left for at least 3 months, as the fruit shrinks and more juice seeps into the brandy.

Ingredients
450g/1lb/scant 3¼ cups ripe black cherries
100g/3½oz/½ cup caster sugar
2–3 drops almond essence
350ml/12fl oz/1½ cups brandy

Remove all the cherry stalks, then wash and dry the fruit. Prick each cherry all over with a sterilized needle or a wooden cocktail stick.

Layer the cherries with the sugar in a large, sterilized preserving jar or lidded jar. Add the almond essence, then pour in the brandy. Seal the jar and shake well.

Keep in a cool, dark place, gently inverting the jar once a day for 1 week, then leave it undisturbed for at least 3 months before using, to allow the flavours to develop.

Line a funnel or nylon sieve with a double layer of muslin and strain the brandy through it into a sterilized bottle. (The brandy will have taken on a deep, rich burgundy colour from the cherries.) Seal the bottle and label it.

The brandy is now ready to use as a liqueur, or as part of a long cocktail with lots of ice. Serve the cherries on a pile of meringues and cream, à la Eton Mess – fantastic!

RATAFIA

This old-fashioned recipe was originally made with wild cherries, but any red or black cultivated varieties can be used. The liqueur is the most glorious dark, ruby red.

Ingredients
700g/1lb 9oz/6¾ cups ripe black cherries
225g/8oz/1½ cups fresh or frozen raspberries
225g/8oz/1¼ cups caster sugar
700ml/1¼ pints/3 cups brandy
A large sprig of fresh coriander
1 large cinnamon stick

Remove all the cherry stalks, then wash and dry the fruit. Using a cherry-stoner, remove the stones from enough cherries to give 40g/1½oz/scant ¼ cup. Reserve these for later use.

Put the stoned and un-stoned cherries into a large, non-metallic bowl and carefully mash with a potato masher. Transfer the pulp into a large, sterilized preserving jar or lidded jar. Pick over the raspberries, removing any leaves, then crush with the potato masher. Add the pulp to the jar. Cover with the lid and leave for 4 days, stirring twice or three times daily.

On the fourth day, crack open the reserved cherry stones with a nutcracker and extract the kernels. Blanch these in boiling water and skin them.

Add the sugar to the fruit in the jar and stir until completely dissolved. Stir in the skinned kernels with the brandy, coriander and cinnamon. Cover the jar again and leave in a cool, dark place to infuse for 1 month.

When the liqueur is ready, strain through a nylon sieve or large plastic funnel, lined with two layers of muslin, into a large sterilized jug, discarding the coriander and cinnamon. Allow the liquid to drain through the muslin, then squeeze the pulp until every drop of liquid is extracted. Discard the pulp and pour the ratafia into a clean, sterilized, screw-capped bottle. Seal tightly, label and store in a cool, dark place for at least another 3 months before drinking.

ANGELICA RATAFIA

A delicious liqueur made with fresh angelica, or 'herb of the angels', which is a lovely plant to grow in the garden. It grows wild in most northern countries of Europe and also in the Pyrenees. In the United States, it is also a plant of the most northern areas. Cut the stems in late summer with scissors.

Ingredients

- 225g/8oz freshly cut angelica stems
- 600ml/1 pint/2½ cups brandy
- 175g/6oz/scant 1 cup caster sugar
- 4 tablespoons water

Wash and dry then cut the stems into small pieces and place in a large, sterilized preserving jar or lidded jar. Cover with the brandy, then seal with a lid and store in a cool, dark place for 2–3 months.

When you are ready to strain the liqueur, stir the caster sugar and water in a small pan over a gentle heat until the sugar has completely dissolved, then bring to the boil. Boil for 1 minute, then leave until completely cold.

Strain the brandy through a nylon sieve or funnel, lined with two layers of muslin, into a sterilized jug. Stir in the sugar syrup, then pour into a sterilized bottle with a screw-cap. Seal tightly, label and store in a cool, dark place until you wish to drink it.

SLOE GIN

Sloes are the fruit of the spiky blackthorn, one of the wild ancestors of many varieties of cultivated plums. The small, dark, round fruits appear in autumn, and tradition has it that they should be picked after the first frost, when they yield more juice. I have found that picking them at their best and freezing them overnight has the same effect. Make sure you use perfect sloes with unbroken skins, or your sloe gin will end up cloudy.

There are numerous recipes for this superb liqueur, the amount of sugar varying with the recipe, from 50g/2¾oz/¼ cup to 350g/12oz/1¾ cups. It really is a matter of individual taste, but I suggest you start by using 100g/3½oz/½ cup. You can then add more, if you wish, when re-bottling after 3 months.

Ingredients

450g/1lb/scant 4 cups unblemished sloes

100g/3½oz/½ cup caster sugar

About 700ml/1¼ pints/3 cups gin

Wash the sloes, discarding leaves and stalks, then dry and freeze overnight.

Next day, thaw the sloes enough to allow you to prick the flesh several times with a sterilized needle or a wooden cocktail stick, then drop them into a large preserving jar or lidded jar.

Add the sugar, then pour in the gin, reserving the bottle for later use. Seal tightly and invert several times to distribute the sugar and start it dissolving.

Leave to infuse in a cool, dark place for at least 3 months, shaking every day for a month. After 3 months, strain the gin through a nylon sieve or large funnel, lined with two layers of muslin, into a sterilized jug. Decant back into the original gin bottle. Screw on the cap and continue to store in a cool, dark place for the following Christmas.

As well as a superb liqueur for drinking neat, sloe gin can be used as a base for various cocktails, such as Sloe Gin Fizz: mix 1 measure of sloe gin with 1 teaspoon lemon juice and soda water to taste. For a wonderful aperitif, add a generous glug of sloe gin to a glass of Champagne or sparkling wine. Try adding sloe gin to poached plums, figs or quinces, to fruit pies and crumbles, or to fruit sauces.

VARIATION

Damson or Plum Gin

Damsons can be found wild in British and European woods and hedgerows, as can the bullace or wild plum. Both make a superb liqueur using the recipe opposite, as do the cultivated fruits. Unlike sloes, you can enjoy the strained fruit with ice cream or yoghurt.

Sloe, Damson or Plum Vodka

Use vodka instead of gin and make as described opposite. The vodka-soaked damsons and plums can be eaten too.

APRICOT BRANDY

Peaches and nectarines can be used instead of apricots, but always use ripe fruit. Drink this as a delicious liqueur, or use to flavour apricot pudding, or cakes.

Ingredients
450g/1lb fresh, ripe apricots
225g/8oz/1⅛ cups caster sugar
600ml/1 pint/2½ cups brandy

Wash the apricots, discarding any leaves and stalks, then dry them. Halve them, then cut into small pieces, reserving the stones. Crack these with nutcrackers, and remove the kernels. Crush the kernels.

Put the chopped apricots into a large, sterilized preserving jar or lidded jar and add the crushed kernels and the sugar. Pour in the brandy and cover tightly. Store in a cool, dry place for 1 month, shaking the jar frequently for the first week.

Strain through a nylon sieve or large funnel, lined with two layers of muslin, into a sterilized jug. Pour the apricot-flavoured brandy into a sterilized screw-capped bottle. Seal tightly, label and store for another 3 months before using.

The brandy-soaked apricot pieces can be eaten as a special dessert, mixed into a fruit salad, used in ice creams, or as a filling for sweet pancakes and meringues.

ORANGE WINE WITH BRANDY

Serve this well chilled as an aperitif. For a special occasion, pour it into a punch bowl and float a few nasturtium flowers on the top.

Ingredients

1kg/2¼lb thin-skinned oranges
225g/8oz/1⅛ cups caster sugar
1 litre/1¾ pints/4 cups dry white wine
150ml/¼ pint/⅔ cup brandy

Scrub the oranges, then warm in a low oven for a few minutes so that they give out more juice. Cut each into six pieces, without peeling them. Put them into a large preserving jar or lidded jar and pour in the wine. Cover closely and leave in a cool, dark place for 7–10 days.

Strain into a large saucepan, pressing the oranges gently before discarding them. Add the sugar and heat gently, stirring all the time until it has dissolved completely. (Don't allow the wine to come anywhere near boiling point. It should not become more than warm.)

Cool the liquor and add the brandy. Then strain through a nylon sieve or large funnel, lined with two layers of muslin, into a sterilized jug, then into sterilized screw-capped bottles. Seal tightly and label. Store in a cool, dark place for at least another week to mature. Serve chilled with a little soda water.

QUINCE VODKA

If you are lucky enough to have your own quince tree, leave the fruit until it is really ripe and yellow all over before picking. However, if windy or wet weather is threatening, pick the fruit even if it is not quite ripe. Take it inside to ripen.

You need only a couple of good-sized quinces for this delicious liqueur, which I first tasted at the home of a very good friend and brilliant cook.

Ingredients
2 large, unblemished, ripe quinces
75g/2¾oz/generous ⅓ cup caster sugar
700ml/1¼ pints/3 cups vodka

Wash the quinces well, rinsing away any grey fluff that might be on them. Don't peel or core the fruit, just grate into a large, sterilized preserving jar or lidded jar. Add the sugar and the vodka, then seal tightly. Give the jar a gentle shake to help dissolve the sugar, then leave in a cool, dark place for at least 2 months. After 2 months, taste and add more sugar if you want, then leave for another 2 months.

Strain through a nylon sieve or funnel lined with two layers of muslin, then transfer into a sterilized screw-capped bottle (the original vodka bottle is ideal). It is ready to drink, but will improve if kept for longer – a year is not too long. Try adding to apple or quince desserts, poached fruit or fruit sauces.

VARIATION

Quince Gin or Quince Brandy
Substitute gin or brandy for the vodka.

LIMONCELLO

A yummy liqueur, which I first tasted sitting outside a café in Sicily. With the heat of the sun and a very strong espresso, it was fantastic; but it is also delicious in the grey days of winter, served with dessert or cheese.

Another good friend gave me this recipe. She suggests that you increase the sugar to 450g/1lb/2¼ cups if you don't find the liqueur sweet enough.

Ingredients

5 unwaxed lemons
175g/6oz/scant 1 cup granulated sugar
75ml/2½fl oz/5 tbsp water
500ml/18fl oz/generous 2 cups vodka

Prepare at least 1 month before drinking.

Wash the lemons and dry well. Place the sugar and water in a small saucepan and stir over a low heat until the sugar has completely dissolved. (Don't let the syrup come to the boil.) Leave on one side to cool.

Using a potato peeler, remove the zest from the lemons without any pith, which will spoil the flavour as it is bitter. Cut the zest into small pieces.

Place the zest of the lemons into a large, sterilized preserving jar or lidded container. Pour in the vodka and add the cooled sugar syrup. Seal the jar or container and store in a cool, dark place for 30–40 days, shaking twice a week to mix up the contents.

After 30–40 days, strain through a nylon sieve or large funnel, lined with two layers of muslin, into a sterilized screw-capped bottle. Discard the lemon zest. Enjoy after a meal, or with the dessert or cheese course.

(Also illustrated on previous page.)

HAWTHORN FLOWER LIQUEUR

The hawthorn, or 'may', grows throughout Britain and Europe. The United States has other species that can be used in the same way to make this pale, delicately almond-flavoured liqueur – a pleasing drink as well as a flavouring for puddings, cakes and biscuits.

Ingredients

100g/3½oz hawthorn flowers, petals only
700ml/1¼ pints/3 cups brandy
175g/6oz/scant 1 cup caster sugar
4 tablespoons water

Pick the blossoms on a dry day during early summer, using scissors to cut them directly into a container. Try not to include any stalks with the flowers as these will give a bitter quality to the liqueur.

Make sure that the flowers are free of insects, then put them in a large, sterilized preserving jar or lidded jar and cover with the brandy. Seal well and store in a cool, dark place for 2–3 months.

When ready to strain the brandy, stir the caster sugar and water in a saucepan, over a gentle heat, until the sugar has completely dissolved, then bring to the boil. Boil for 1 minute, then strain through a nylon sieve, lined with muslin, into a small bowl and leave to get completely cold.

Strain the brandy through a nylon sieve, lined with a double layer of muslin, into a large sterilized jug. Stir in the sugar syrup to taste, then pour into a sterilized screw-capped bottle. Seal tightly, label and store in a cool, dark place until you want to drink it.

RASPBERRY SHRUB

'Shrub' is another name for a spirit combined with fruit juice and sugar, popularly used in the eighteenth and nineteenth centuries. The word comes from the Arabic word *shurb*, meaning 'drink'.

You can also use loganberries, cloudberries, blueberries, cranberries, blackberries, strawberries and gooseberries – but may need to adapt the amount of sugar at the point of bottling. It is always advisable to add less sugar at the beginning, since you can't remove it when you bottle.

INGREDIENTS
450g/1lb/3 cups fresh
raspberries
100g/3½oz/½ cup caster sugar
600ml/1 pint/2½ cups vodka

Pick over the fruit, removing any leaves, but don't wash. Put it into a large, sterilized preserving jar or lidded jar and sprinkle with the sugar. Press gently with a wooden spoon until the juice begins to run. Pour the vodka over it.

Cover with the lid and leave in a cool, dark place for at least 1 month, turning or shaking the jar every day for the first week. Strain through a large funnel or nylon sieve, lined with two layers of muslin, into a sterilized jug, then transfer to a sterilized screw-capped bottle.

Seal and label, then store in a cool, dark place for another few weeks before drinking. (Also illustrated on pages 112–113.)

VARIATION

Raspberry Brandy or Raspberry Gin
Use brandy or gin instead of vodka and flavour with other soft fruits (see opposite).

BEERS AND ALES

roll out the barrels!

PURE AND SIMPLE

PILSNER

This style is named after the town of Pilsen in the Czech Republic. The name suggests that it is simple, and a look at the ingredients seems to confirm this, but making lager and Pilsner styles is undertaken only by more advanced brewers. In order for this to stay rigidly to style, and indeed for the recommended yeasts to work properly, this brew should be fermented at a much lower temperatures than ale. The beer should then be 'lagered' for a number of weeks. This entails dropping the temperature of the beer from the range at which it was fermented 10–15°C/50–59°F to 1–4°C/33–39°F for at least 6 weeks. If you want to explore something that is like a lager, but easier to brew, try Essex Blonde (page 122).

Follow the process starting on page 52, using:

IN MASH	WEIGHT		
Pilsner Malt	4.75kg		

WATER REQUIRED	VOLUME		
Total Liquor	37 litres/8⅛ gallons/9¾ US gallons		
Mash Liquor	12 litres/2½ gallons/3⅛ US gallons		

IN BOIL	WEIGHT	ALPHA ACID	TIME FROM END
Hallertauer Magnum	21g	11.0%	90 minutes
Protofloc	1 tsp		15 minutes
Saaz	19g	3.0%	10 minutes

STATISTICS			
Expected OG	1045	Colour (EBC)	5.3
Expected FG	1011	Bitterness (IBU)	29.5
Expected ABV	4.4%		

YEAST RECOMMENDATIONS			
DCL – S23	WLP – 800	WY – 2278	

EXTRACT VERSION
MALT EXTRACT REQUIRED
Liquid Pilsner Malt Extract 3kg
Dry Malt Extract 500g

GOLDEN PRIDE

ENGLISH SUMMER ALE

In terms of strict beer style, this is still a best bitter, but I've included it here because it's an increasingly popular style with drinkers. It's light, it's refreshing, but it's not a lager, it's still an ale. It's got lots of British hop character, finished with a classic Golding aroma. There are a number of very popular ales currently on the market which this sits alongside nicely.

Follow the process starting on page 52, using:

IN MASH	WEIGHT		
Pale Ale Malt	4.720kg		

WATER REQUIRED	VOLUME		
Total Liquor	37 litres/8⅛ gallons/9¾ US gallons		
Mash Liquor	12 litres/2½ gallons/3⅛ US gallons		

IN BOIL	WEIGHT	ALPHA ACID	TIME FROM END
UK Target	19g	10.5%	90 minutes
UK Bramling Cross	13g	6%	30 minutes
Protofloc	1 tsp		15 minutes
UK Golding	12g	5.5%	10 minutes

STATISTICS			
Expected FG	1012	Colour (EBC)	10.3
Expected OG	1044	Bitterness (IBU)	33.1
Expected ABV	4.3%		

YEAST RECOMMENDATIONS			
	DCL – S04	WLP – 023	WY – 1028

EXTRACT VERSION
Malt Extract Required

Light Liquid Malt Extract	3kg
Dried Malt Extract	450g

SAIS WHO?

SAISON

This is a classic farmhouse beer from the Walloon region in Belgium. It was traditionally brewed as a drink for farm workers, to refresh them after a day in the fields. It doesn't just use hops to flavour it, and can have a wide range of herbs and spices added to provide interest. The yeasts in this brew will give it some very different flavours, and even the same strain will change within the optimum temperature range.

Follow the process starting on page 52, using:

IN MASH	WEIGHT
Lager Malt	3kg
Munich Malt	1.1kg
Torrified Wheat	240g
Medium Crystal Malt	210g
Belgian Biscuit Malt	160g

WATER REQUIRED	VOLUME
Total Liquor	38 litres/8¼ gallons/10 US gallons
Mash Liquor	13 litres/3 gallons/3½ US gallons

IN BOIL	WEIGHT	ALPHA ACID	TIME FROM END
German Brewer's Gold	19g	7%	90 minutes
UK Golding	10g	5.5%	30 minutes
Star Anise	10g		20 minutes
Protofloc	1 tsp		15 minutes
Slovenian Styrian Golding	12g	4.5%	10 minutes
Crushed Coriander Seed	20g		10 minutes

STATISTICS			
Expected OG	1049	Colour (EBC)	18.1
Expected FG	1009	Bitterness (IBU)	22.4
Expected ABV	5.3%		

YEAST RECOMMENDATIONS		
DCL – S33	WLP – 566	WY – 3724

ESSEX BLONDE

BRITISH BLONDE

This is an attempt to create a British-style beer with Czech and German hops, giving it a malty base and some body but finishing it off with the crisp, clean and classic hops that are used in continental lagers. This is also a style that many commercial brewers are developing: it is proving popular, appealing to the lager drinker looking to try real ale. It's not too dark, it's not too heavy and the aroma and bitterness has got a familiarity to it.

Follow the process starting on page 52, using:

IN MASH	WEIGHT		
Pale Ale Malt	4.215kg		
Light Crystal Malt	125g		
Torrified Wheat	125g		

WATER REQUIRED	VOLUME		
Total Liquor	36.5 litres/8⅛ gallons/9¾ US gallons		
Mash Liquor	11 litres/3¼ gallons/4 US gallons		

IN BOIL	WEIGHT	ALPHA ACID	TIME FROM END
Northern Brewer	28g	8%	90 minutes
Northern Brewer	12g	8%	30 minutes
Protofloc	1 tsp		15 minutes
Tettnang	12g	4.5%	10 minutes

STATISTICS			
Expected OG	1041	Bitterness (IBU)	37.7
Expected FG	1011	Colour (EBC)	12.4
Expected ABV	4%		

YEAST RECOMMENDATIONS			
	DCL – S04	WLP – 022	WY – 1318

FLAMING JUNE

IPA

During the British occupation of India, one enterprising brewer decided to take advantage of the long voyage to India. Large numbers of such ships were often empty, having delivered their goods from India to Britain. The brewer therefore decided to offer a beer that matured on the boat to India rather than being cellared in Britain. This saved costs for him and became very popular with expats. Ever since, IPA (India Pale Ale) has come to mean a highly hopped beer with a moderate alcohol content. It might need a longer than usual maturing period due to the hop levels. A container going to India is said to help.

Follow the process starting on page 52, using:

IN MASH	WEIGHT
Pale Ale Malt	5.22kg
Medium Crystal Malt	415g

WATER REQUIRED	VOLUME
Total Liquor	38 litres/8¼ gallons/10 US gallons
Mash Liquor	14 litres/3⅛ gallons/3¾ US gallons

IN BOIL	WEIGHT	ALPHA ACID	TIME FROM END
UK Admiral	31g	14.5%	90 minutes
Protofloc	1 tsp		15 minutes
UK First Gold	13g	8%	10 minutes

STATISTICS			
Expected OG	1052	Colour (EBC)	22.4
Expected FG	1041	Bitterness (IBU)	56.1
Expected ABV	5%		

YEAST RECOMMENDATIONS			
	DCL – S04	WLP – 023	WY – 1028

EXTRACT VERSION
Malt Extract Required

		Steeped Grains	
Light Liquid Malt Extract	3kg	UK Medium Crystal Malt	415g
Light Dried Malt Extract	700g		

PALE RIDER

AIPA

IPA (India Pale Ale) as become such an iconic and classic style of beer that it has its own regional variations. A traditional IPA uses classic British hops; there are variations using American hops (like this one – AIPA) or New Zealand hops. This one has some big citrus flavours, mainly pink grapefruit, giving it a very distinctive flavour. IPAs are a popular home-brew style and many people take them to their bitter and alcoholic extremes in what are termed 'imperial' IPAs.

Follow the process starting on page 52, using:

IN MASH	WEIGHT
Pale Ale Malt	5.73kg
Medium Crystal Malt	365g

WATER REQUIRED	VOLUME
Total Liquor	38 litres/8¼ gallons/10 US gallons
Mash Liquor	15 litres/3¼ gallons/4 US gallons

IN BOIL	WEIGHT	ALPHA ACID	TIME FROM END
US Columbus (Tomahawk)	24g	15.5%	90 minutes
Protofloc	1 tsp		15 minutes
US Chinook	19g	10.5%	10 minutes

STATISTICS			
Expected OG	1056	Colour (EBC)	21.8
Expected FG	1014	Bitterness (IBU)	50.7
Expected ABV	5.7%		

YEAST RECOMMENDATIONS		
DCL – S04	WLP – 023	WY – 1028

EXTRACT VERSION

Malt Extract Required
Light Liquid Malt Extract 3kg
Light Dried Malt Extract 1.05kg

Steeped Grains
Medium Crystal Malt 365g

PACIFIC PARTNER

NZ IPA

This gives a variation on the same IPA (India Pale Ale) theme, this time bringing in hops from New Zealand. Some of these, like the NZ Willamette, are the same variety grown in a different climate, but others, like the Nelson Sauvin, are unique in the hop world. The Nelson Sauvin was named in brewery trials when it imparted a suggestion of Sauvignon Blanc to the brew – in other words, almost tart white wine grape flavours and aromas.

Follow the process starting on page 52, using:

IN MASH	WEIGHT		
Pale Ale Malt	5.135kg		
Medium Crystal Malt	260g		
Black Malt	30g		

WATER REQUIRED	VOLUME		
Total Liquor	37.5 litres/8⅛ gallons/9¾ US gallons		
Mash Liquor	13.5 litres/3 gallons/3½ US gallons		

IN BOIL	WEIGHT	ALPHA ACID	TIME FROM END
NZ Pacific	14g	14%	90 minutes
NZ Nelson Sauvin	12g	12.5%	30 minutes
Protofloc	1 tsp		15 minutes
NZ Willamette	8g	7%	10 minutes

STATISTICS			
Expected OG	1050	Colour (EBC)	25
Expected FG	1012	Bitterness (IBU)	40.2
Expected ABV	5%		

YEAST RECOMMENDATIONS			
	DCL – S04	WLP – 023	WY – 1028

EXTRACT VERSION

Malt Extract Required		Steeped Grains	
Liquid Malt Extract	3kg	Medium Crystal Malt	260g
Dried Malt Extract	650g	Black Malt	30g

MINUTE WALTZ

VIENNA LAGER

The Vienna lager is one of the styles which demonstrates that not all lagers are pale: it still retains the crisp, classic German and Czech hop flavours, with little or no aroma. It differs by having a little more body and a little malt sweetness. It's a style that nearly died out but was revived in the late 1800s by Austrian migrants to Mexico. This will need lagering as described in the recipe for Pure and Simple (page 118).

Follow the process starting on page 52, using:

IN MASH	WEIGHT		
Vienna Malt	4.65kg		
Munich Malt	570g		
Black Malt	57g		

WATER REQUIRED	VOLUME		
Total Liquor	37 litres/8⅛ gallons/9¾ US gallons		
Mash Liquor	13 litres/3 gallons/3½ US gallons		

IN BOIL	WEIGHT	ALPHA ACID	TIME FROM END
German Tettnang	42g	4.5%	90 minutes
Protofloc	1 tsp		15 minutes

STATISTICS			
Expected OG	1049	Colour (EBC)	26.1
Expected FG	1012	Bitterness (IBU)	21.9
Expected ABV	4.9%		

YEAST RECOMMENDATIONS			
	DCL – S23	WLP – 830	WY – 2308

DOUBLE TROUBLE

DUBBEL

The Belgian brewing tradition is as different to brewing culture elsewhere in the world as it could be. One could be mistaken for thinking that Belgian brewers were mad scientists stuck in laboratories, but many of the traditions come from monasteries where monks used products brought from around the world to create their beer. This particular style is all about the malt's character coming through; the variety in the big grain bill provides all the aroma and flavours. The hops in this brew are there principally to balance the malt's sweetness, and not as a distinct flavour component.

Follow the process starting on page 52, using:

IN MASH	WEIGHT
Belgian Pilsen Malt	4.95kg
Belgian Biscuit Malt	375g
Belgian Aromatic Malt	275g

WATER REQUIRED	VOLUME
Total Liquor	37.5 litres/8¼ gallons/10 US gallons
Mash Liquor	14 litres/3 gallons/3½ US gallons

IN BOIL	WEIGHT	ALPHA ACID	TIME FROM END
Sugar-Candi Sugar Amber	600g		
German Northern Brewer	24g	8%	90 minutes
Protofloc	1 tsp		15 minutes

STATISTICS			
Expected OG	1060	Colour (EBC)	31.9
Expected FG	1010	Bitterness (IBU)	21.2
Expected ABV	6.6%		

YEAST RECOMMENDATIONS		
DCL – S33	WLP – 500	WY – 1214

BOLD AS BRASS

BITTER

This is an ordinary bitter, not as strong as a best bitter, but not as weak as a mild. It maintains the hop bitterness that milds lack. The style has been brewed for many years as the standard pub drink – a session ale. It's very drinkable, with an interesting hop profile. Look out for the spicy blackcurrant notes imparted by the Bramling Cross hops.

Follow the process starting on page 52, using:

IN MASH	WEIGHT		
Pale Ale Malt	3.62kg		
Torrified Wheat	260g		
Medium Crystal Malt	100g		
Black Malt	65g		

WATER REQUIRED	VOLUME		
Total Liquor	36 litres/8 gallons/9½ US gallons		
Mash Liquor	10 litres/2 gallons/2½ US gallons		

IN BOIL	WEIGHT	ALPHA ACID	TIME FROM END
UK Northdown	19g	8.0%	90 minutes
UK First Gold	13g	8.0%	45 minutes
Protofloc	1 tsp		15 minutes
UK Bramling Cross	10g	6.0%	10 minutes

STATISTICS			
Expected OG	1037	Colour (EBC)	27
Expected FG	1009	Bitterness (IBU)	32
Expected ABV	3.7%		

YEAST RECOMMENDATIONS			
	DCL – S04	WLP – 007	WY – 1026

BANK STREET BEST

BEST BITTER

This is a best bitter, a classic British style of beer with a taste profile and alcohol content that allows you to drink more than one. Traditionally served using hand pumps and often described as a 'real ale' (depending on how it's made and served), this was at one point a drink of choice for working men in pubs. The advent of smokeless fuels led to lighter coloured malts, which allowed for the development of lighter beers. This is made in the style which developed from the great breweries of Burton-on-Trent.

Follow the process starting on page 52, using:

IN MASH	WEIGHT		
Pale Ale Malt	4.85kg		
Crystal Malt	200g		
Chocolate Malt	45g		

WATER REQUIRED	VOLUME		
Total Liquor	37 litres/8⅛ gallons/9¾ US gallons		
Mash Liquor	13 litres/2¾ gallons/3¼ US gallons		

IN BOIL	WEIGHT	ALPHA ACID	TIME FROM END
UK Challenger	22g	7.0%	90 minutes
UK Bramling Cross	19g	6.0%	20 minutes
Protofloc	1 tsp		15 minutes
UK Golding	16g	4.6%	5 minutes

STATISTICS			
Expected OG	1047	Colour (EBC)	24.9
Expected FG	1012	Bitterness (IBU)	27
Expected ABV	4.6%		

YEAST RECOMMENDATIONS			
	DCL – S04	WLP – 026	WY – 1318

EXTRACT VERSION

Malt Extract Required		Steeped Grains	
Light Liquid Malt Extract	3kg	Crystal Malt	200g
Light Dried Malt Extract	500g	Chocolate Malt	45g

THE RACONTEUR

WHEAT BEER

This wheat beer is in the Belgian tradition and is a fresh and light brew. It's another style that doesn't use the hops alone to add alternative flavours to the malt. As with many other Belgian styles, the yeast is an important factor in this.

Follow the process starting on page 52, using:

IN MASH	WEIGHT		
Torrified Wheat	2.48kg		
Lager Malt	2.48kg		

WATER REQUIRED	VOLUME		
Total Liquor	37 litres/8⅛ gallons/9¾ US gallons		
Mash Liquor	12.5 litres/2¾ gallons/3¼ US gallons		

IN BOIL	WEIGHT	ALPHA ACID	TIME FROM END
UK Golding	31g	5.5%	90 minutes
Protofloc	1 tsp		15 minutes
Coriander Seed	20g		10 minutes
Orange Peel (Bitter)	15g		End

STATISTICS			
Expected OG	1046 SG	Colour (EBC)	7.9
Expected FG	1011 SG	Bitterness (IBU)	13.9
Expected ABV	4.6%		

YEAST RECOMMENDATIONS			
	DCL – S33	WLP – 400	WY – 3944

OVERLORD

EXTRA-SPECIAL BITTER

The ESB (extra-special bitter) style is, to a certain extent, the British 'bitter' style writ large. What best bitters have, ESBs have in bagfuls: lots of fruit and malt flavours, slightly more bitterness and a higher alcohol content. Unlike their best bitter and ordinary bitter counterparts, these are not session ales. They are, as they say, special; not the kind of beer for a cheeky pint at lunchtime. More than anything, they deserve more time in order for you to enjoy the flavours and aromas.

Follow the process starting on page 52, using:

IN MASH	WEIGHT		
Pale Ale Malt	4.93kg		
Medium Crystal Malt	290g		
Torrified Wheat	210g		
Chocolate Malt	115g		

WATER REQUIRED	VOLUME
Total Liquor	37.5 litres/8¼ gallons/10 US gallons
Mash Liquor	14 litres/3⅛ gallons/3¾ US gallons

IN BOIL	WEIGHT	ALPHA ACID	TIME FROM END
White Sugar	115g		
UK Target	19g	10.5%	90 minutes
UK Bramling Cross	18g	6.0%	30 minutes
UK Golding	13g	5.5%	30 minutes
Protofloc	1 tsp		15 minutes
UK Golding	14g	5.5%	10 minutes

STATISTICS			
Expected OG	1053	Colour (EBC)	37.8
Expected FG	1013	Bitterness (IBU)	40.3
Expected ABV	5.3%		

YEAST RECOMMENDATIONS		
DCL – S04	WLP – 026	WY – 1768

ROOFER'S REVENGE

MODERN MILD

Mild has, in recent years, come to mean a style of beer that is not strong and not highly hopped. There's nothing wrong with this, and there are some fantastic-tasting brews in this style. It's not the original meaning, but it's a nice style. It lends itself to an easy to drink, tasty brew for those who like their malt flavours. The low gravity means that this will condition quickly, but it will not keep for as long as stronger brews.

Follow the process starting on page 52, using:

IN MASH	WEIGHT
Pale Ale Malt	3.1kg
Medium Crystal Malt	210g
Chocolate Malt	105g
Torrified Wheat	100g

WATER REQUIRED	VOLUME
Total Liquor	35.5 litres/7½ gallons/9¼ US gallons
Mash Liquor	9 litres/1 gallons/2⅜ US gallons

IN BOIL	WEIGHT	ALPHA ACID	TIME FROM END
UK Challenger	18g	7%	90 minutes
UK Fuggle	10g	4.5%	90 minutes
Protofloc	1 tsp		15 minutes
UK Fuggle	10g	4.5%	10 minutes

STATISTICS			
Expected OG	1032	Colour (EBC)	32.9
Expected FG	1009	Bitterness (IBU)	23.6
Expected ABV	3.1%		

YEAST RECOMMENDATIONS			
	DCL – S04	WLP – 023	WY – 1028

THE MIDLANDER
"THERE CAN ONLY BE ONE" VINTAGE MILD

This mild recipe is more in line with the milds of yesteryear: it's not highly hopped, but the gravity is significantly higher than a modern mild. Historically, 'mild' simply meant that it had not been aged: it was new beer, as opposed to stale beer. This is something of a British institution, and was one of the best-selling beer styles until the 1950s. It remained popular in the Midlands even when many other British regions had switched their preferences to lager and bitter.

Follow the process starting on page 52, using:

IN MASH	WEIGHT		
Pale Ale Malt	4.7kg		
Medium Crystal Malt	795g		
Chocolate Malt	115g		

WATER REQUIRED	VOLUME		
Total Liquor	37 litres/8¼ gallons/10 US gallons		
Mash Liquor	14 litres/3⅛ gallons/3¾ US gallons		

IN BOIL	WEIGHT	ALPHA ACID	TIME FROM END
UK Challenger	22g	7%	90 minutes
Protofloc	1 tsp		15 minutes
UK Golding	10g	5.5%	10 minutes

STATISTICS			
Expected OG	1051	Colour (EBC)	46.7
Expected FG	1013	Bitterness (IBU)	20.4
Expected ABV	5%		

YEAST RECOMMENDATIONS			
DCL – S04	WLP – 023	WY – 1028	

KENTUCKY PLAIN

VANILLA BOURBON PORTER

This is a playful variation on a traditional porter. The addition of the vanilla notes to the roast gives the drink a softness, which is counterbalanced by the bourbon flavour. The vanilla flavour comes from two whole chopped vanilla beans added to a second fermenter. Once the main fermentation is over, rack to the second fermenter and leave the brew there to infuse with vanilla for 1 week. Add 345ml/12fl oz of good bourbon to the third fermenter along with the priming sugar, then bottle.

Follow the process starting on page 52, using:

IN MASH	WEIGHT		
Pale Ale Malt	3.925kg		
Torrified Wheat	310g		
Dark Crystal Malt	290g		
Chocolate Malt	260g		

WATER REQUIRED	VOLUME
Total Liquor	37 litres/8⅛ gallons/9¾ US gallons
Mash Liquor	12 litres/2¾ gallons/3¼ US gallons

IN BOIL	WEIGHT	ALPHA ACID	TIME FROM END
UK Northdown	21g	8%	90 minutes
UK Target	10g	10.5%	90 minutes
UK Northdown	10g	8%	30 minutes
Protofloc	1 tsp		15 minutes

STATISTICS			
Expected OG	1044	Colour (EBC)	57.2
Expected FG	1012	Bitterness (IBU)	38.2
Expected ABV	4.3%		

YEAST RECOMMENDATIONS			
	DCL – S04	WLP – 013	WY – 1275

DUBH GLAS

PORTER

Named after the Gaelic for 'dark water', this porter certainly is. The distinction between porter and stout is hard to pin down: even Guiness Extra was a porter until its name was changed in 1840. There are many theories about the origins of the drink, many of them involving the blending of stale beer with mild to create a cheaper, but robust drink. London is often cited as its origin, the beer being aged in vats by the brewery as opposed to the publican, which was the practice at the time.

Follow the process starting on page 52, using:

IN MASH	WEIGHT		
Pale Ale Malt	4.31kg		
Medium Crystal Malt	425g		
Torrified Wheat	380g		
Roasted Barley	240g		

WATER REQUIRED	VOLUME		
Total Liquor	37 litres/8⅛ gallons/9¾ US gallons		
Mash Liquor	13 litres/3 gallons/3½ US gallons		

IN BOIL	WEIGHT	ALPHA ACID	TIME FROM END
UK Target	21g	10.5%	90 minutes
UK Progress	8g	5.5%	45 minutes
Protofloc	1 tsp		15 minutes
UK Golding	15g	5.5%	10 minutes

STATISTICS			
Expected OG	1049	Colour (EBC)	67.6
Expected FG	1013	Bitterness (IBU)	32.9
Expect ABV	4.8%		

YEAST RECOMMENDATIONS			
	DCL — S04	WLP — 013	WY — 1275

BLACK GOLD

IRISH STOUT

Stout is not the drink we know today: it originally referred to a stronger beer. The inclusion of roasted unmalted barley came about during the Napoleonic wars, when malt was taxed for the first time. Adding an untaxed ingredient kept costs down. The dominance of Irish breweries in the stout market is more recent: in the First World War, restrictions were made in Britain on both the strength of beer and the amount of energy used to make it. Roasted barley therefore became more difficult to use, and the high gravity of traditional stout could not be maintained. The Irish breweries remained unrestricted and went on to dominate the market.

Follow the process starting on page 52, using:

IN MASH	WEIGHT		
Pale Ale Malt	4.45kg		
Roasted Barley	465g		

WATER REQUIRED	VOLUME		
Total Liquor	37 litres/8⅛ gallons/9¾ US gallons		
Mash Liquor	12 litres/2¾ gallons/3¼ US gallons		

IN BOIL	WEIGHT	ALPHA ACID	TIME FROM END
UK Target	25g	10.5%	90 minutes
Protofloc	1 tsp		15 minutes
UK Fuggle	12g	4.5%	10 minutes

STATISTICS			
Expected OG	1045	Colour (EBC)	94.3
Expected FG	1011	Bitterness (IBU)	33.2
Expected ABV	4.6%		

YEAST RECOMMENDATIONS			
	DCL – S04	WLP – 006	WY – 1026

EXTRACT VERSION

Malt Extract Required		Steeped Grains	
Light Liquid Malt Extract	3kg	Roasted Barley	465g
Light Dried Malt Extract	150g		

NURSEMAID

MILK STOUT

This is a traditional sweet stout. As the name suggests, it was prescribed to nursing mothers many moons ago. The sweetness and the name come from the lactose sugar added to the boil, which is derived from milk. The yeast is unable to ferment this and it leaves a residual sweetness.

Follow the process starting on page 52, using:

IN MASH	WEIGHT
Pale Ale Malt	4.13kg
Torrified Wheat	620g
Roasted Barley	215g
Chocolate Malt	210g

WATER REQUIRED	VOLUME
Total Liquor	37.5 litres/8¼ gallons/10 US gallons
Mash Liquor	13 litres/3 gallons/3½ US gallons

IN BOIL	WEIGHT	ALPHA ACID	TIME FROM END
Sugar: Lactose	440g		90 minutes
UK Challenger	27g	7%	90 minutes
Protofloc	1 tsp		15 minutes

STATISTICS			
Expected OG	1053	Colour (EBC)	80.1
Expected FG	1018	Bitterness (IBU)	21.2
Expected ABV	4.7%		

YEAST RECOMMENDATIONS		
DCL – S04	WLP – 006	WY – 1026

CHERRY CREEK

CHERRY BEER

This is a wheat-based drink, with many of the characteristics you would expect from a cherry beer. The cherry addition is made after the boil as soon as the wort is cooled to 75°C/167°F. The cherries should be crushed and added with their stones to the fermenter. This is made easier if the cherries are held in a muslin bag, which is steeped in the wort before being turned out into the fermenter. The final volume of this beer will be less than the full amount, due to the cherry pulp. The Pectolase is added to stop the fruit sugars setting like jam, and to aid clarification.

Follow the process starting on page 52, using:

IN MASH	WEIGHT		
Lager Malt	2.3kg		
Wheat Malt	2.2kg		

WATER REQUIRED	VOLUME		
Total Liquor	36.5 litres/8 gallons/9⅝ US gallons		
Mash Liquor	11 litres/2½ gallons/3 US gallons		

IN BOIL	WEIGHT	ALPHA ACID	TIME FROM END
UK Challenger	22g	7.0%	90 minutes
Protofloc	1 tsp		15 minutes
Sour Cherries (Morello)	4kg		When cooling
Pectolase	20g		In fermenter

STATISTICS			
Expected OG	1062	Colour (EBC)	Red: not on scale
Expected FG	1015	Bitterness (IBU)	9.8
Expected ABV	6.3%		

YEAST RECOMMENDATIONS			
	DCL — S33	WLP — 400	WY — 1388

EXTRACT VERSION
Malt Extract Required

Light Liquid Malt Extract	1.5kg
Wheat Liquid Malt Extract	1.5kg

HUBBLE BUBBLE

CHOCOLATE STOUT

The inclusion of chocolate in stout is something of a new phenomenon. The flavour has always had elements that are reminiscent of coffee and indeed chocolate, and in order to emphasize this, brewers are now adding chocolate to their brews. You can use chocolate, but this can get very messy and add oils that can spoil head retention. This recipe uses cocoa powder to add the flavours in concentrated form.

Follow the process starting on page 52, using:

IN MASH	WEIGHT		
Pale Ale Malt	3.6kg		
Chocolate Malt	415g		
Torrified Wheat	260g		
Roasted Barley	200g		
Medium Crystal Malt	200g		

WATER REQUIRED	VOLUME		
Total Liquor	37 litres/8⅛ gallons/9¾ US gallons		
Mash Liquor	12 litres/2½ gallons/3 US gallons		

IN BOIL	WEIGHT	ALPHA ACID	TIME FROM END
UK Challenger	38g	7%	90 minutes
Protofloc	1 tsp		15 minutes
Cocoa Powder	45g		10 minutes

STATISTICS			
Expected OG	1043	Colour (EBC)	99.9
Expected FG	1011	Bitterness (IBU)	31.5
Expect ABV	4.1%		

YEAST RECOMMENDATIONS			
	DCL – S04	WLP – 006	WY – 1026

THE SMOKEHOUSE

SMOKED BEER

Rauchbier is a tradition kept alive by some very small, very old breweries in Bamberg in Germany. They use malt dried over beechwood smoke, which gives a smoky flavour to the malt. A number of Scottish brews use peat-smoked malt. Rauch malt can be used to make up most of the grain bill, but peat-smoked malt can be very overpowering in all but very small additions. This is a lager and should be lagered as described in Pure and Simple (page 118).

Follow the process starting on page 52, using:

IN MASH	WEIGHT		
Rauch Malt	3.24kg		
Vienna Malt	1.16kg		
Munich Malt	1.16kg		
Chocolate Malt	230g		

WATER REQUIRED	VOLUME
Total Liquor	38 litres/8¼ gallons/10 US gallons
Mash Liquor	14.5 litres/3⅛ gallons/3¾ US gallons

IN BOIL	WEIGHT	ALPHA ACID	TIME FROM END
German Hallertauer Magnum	32g	11%	In mash
Protofloc	1 tsp		15 minutes

STATISTICS			
Expected OG	1054	Colour (EBC)	49.1
Expected FG	1016	Bitterness (IBU)	27.7
Expected ABV	5%		

YEAST RECOMMENDATIONS		
DCL – T58	WLP – 820	WY – 2633

PADDINGTON BEER

ORANGE HEFEWEIZEN

For those of you unfamiliar with a certain Peruvian bear, this brew has oranges in it. Whilst Pale Rider (see page 125) has grapefruit flavours from the hops, this beer has a marmalade orange flavour provided by half the rind and all the pulp from five oranges. You must include only the orange part of the rind because the white part will impart an extremely bitter flavour to the brew. This should be brought up to 75°C/167°F in 2 litres of water 20 minutes before the end of the boil and then left to cool. The liquid and solids should be added to the fermenter before pitching the yeast.

Follow the process starting on page 52, using:

IN MASH	WEIGHT		
Wheat Malt	4.9kg		
Roasted Wheat Malt	30g		

WATER REQUIRED	VOLUME		
Total Liquor	37 litres/8⅛ gallons/9¾ US gallons		
Mash Liquor	12 litres/2½ gallons/3 US gallons		

IN BOIL	WEIGHT	ALPHA ACID	TIME FROM END
German Hallertauer	10g	11%	90 minutes
German Hallertauer Mittlefruh	5g	5%	15 minutes
Protofloc	1 tsp		15 minutes

STATISTICS			
Expected OG	1045	Colour (EBC)	13.9
Expected FG	1012	Bitterness (IBU)	13.3
Expected ABV	4.3%		

YEAST RECOMMENDATIONS			
	DCL – T58	WLP – 300	WY – 3333

EXTRACT VERSION

Malt Extract Required		Steeped Grains	
Liquid Wheat Malt Extract	3kg	Roasted Wheat Malt 30g	
Dry Wheat Malt Extract	450g		

SANTA'S LITTLE HELPER

SPICED CHRISTMAS ALE

There's a style of beer for every time of the year, and Christmas is no exception. A traditional British bitter is used as a base, and lots of Christmas flavours added to make you feel festive – a mulled beer, as it were.

Follow the process starting on page 52, using:

IN MASH	WEIGHT		
Pale Ale Malt	4.5kg		
Medium Crystal Malt	465g		
Roasted Barley	45g		

WATER REQUIRED	VOLUME		
Total Liquor	37 litres/8⅛ gallons/9¾ US gallons		
Mash Liquor	12.5 litres/2¾ gallons/3¼ US gallons		

IN BOIL	WEIGHT	ALPHA ACID	TIME FROM END
UK Challenger	19g	7%	90 minutes
UK Fuggle	12g	4.5%	30 minutes
Star Anise	10g		20 minutes
Protofloc	1 tsp		15 minutes
Cinnamon Sticks	3 sticks		10 minutes
Chopped Fresh Ginger	30g		10 minutes

STATISTICS			
Expected OG	1046	Colour (EBC)	33.2
Expected FG	1012	Bitterness (IBU)	19.7
Expected ABV	4.5%		

YEAST RECOMMENDATIONS			
	DCL – S04	WLP – 028	WY – 1469

EXTRACT VERSION

Malt Extract Required		Steeped Grains	
Liquid Light Malt Extract	3kg	Medium Crystal Malt	465g
Dry Light Malt Extract	300g	Roasted Barley	45g

MINE'S A HALF

BARLEY WINE (HALF EXTRACT)

This is not strictly a beer but a barley wine, brewed in exactly the same way as a beer but is significantly stronger. Ordinarily this would be made with a very large grain bill and sparged with a high volume of water to extract the sugars . This would then be boiled for a very long time to force off the water; a fan on the top helps with the evaporation. I've assumed, though, that you don't want to have your boiler running for 6–8 hours, so this recipes uses malt extract, added to a full-mash brew of a normal length. Add the malt extract to the wort, as for extract brewing (see page 52). This will require a larger yeast starter than usual, or two packets of yeast.

Follow the process starting on page 52, using:

IN MASH	WEIGHT		
Pale Ale Malt	4.26kg		
Medium Crystal Malt	820g		

WATER REQUIRED	VOLUME		
Total Liquor	37 litres/8⅛ gallons/9¾ US gallons		
Mash Liquor	13 litres/2¾ gallons/3¼ US gallons		

IN BOIL	WEIGHT	ALPHA ACID	TIME FROM END
Extract-Light Liquid Malt Extract	3kg		
Demerara Sugar	930g		
UK Target	46g	10.5%	90 minutes
Protofloc	1 tsp		15 minutes
UK Golding	15g	5.5%	10 minutes

STATISTICS			
Expected OG	1098	Colour (EBC)	34.5
Expected FG	1015	Bitterness (IBU)	50.1
Expected ABV	11.2%		

YEAST RECOMMENDATIONS			
	DCL – S33	WLP – 099	WY – 1728

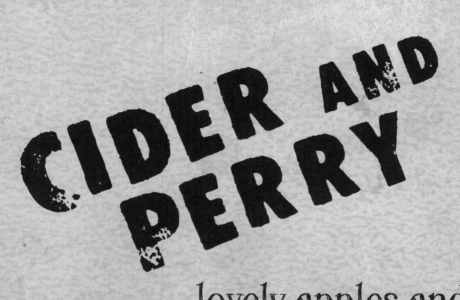

CIDER AND PERRY

lovely apples and pears

3 BASIC CIDERS AND PERRYS

Cider and perry can be made from whatever proportion of apples you have to hand. If you have a choice, though, a mix of the taste qualities (sweet, acidic and bitter) in the proportions listed below will ensure that the cider is to your taste. You can mix and match between apples and pears, depending on what you have available.

Follow the process starting on page 62.

Sweet Cider or Perry
5kg/11lb sweet apples or pears
2.5kg/5.5lb acidic apples or pears
2.5kg/5.5lb bitter apples or pears
Yeast

Medium Cider or Perry
3.75kg/8lb sweet apples or pears
3.75kg/8lb acidic apples or pears
2.5kg/5lb bitter apples or pears
Yeast

Dry Cider or Perry
5kg/11lb acidic apples or pears
2.5kg/5lb sweet apples or pears
2.5kg/5lb bitter apples or pears
Yeast

BLUSH CIDER

A blush cider is slightly sweeter tasting than regular cider, and is red-tinted from the raspberries in the recipe. (Other red soft fruit can be used.) The fruit gives an additional dimension to the flavour, and can make cider containing dessert apples a lot more interesting. Simply mash the raspberries and add them to the juice once it has been extracted from the pomace. This will need a careful first racking to ensure that no raspberry pulp is transferred.

Follow the process starting on page 62.
Ingredients
3.25kg/7lb sweet apples
3.75kg/8lb acidic apples
2.5kg/5lb bitter apples
600g/1lb 5oz/4 cups raspberries
Yeast

MULLED CIDER

This is an ideal cider to make towards the end of the apple season, to mature over the winter. It's ideal served warm, and can be sweetened using honey as you warm it. It's a good recipe for a cider with a higher alcohol content.

Follow the process starting on page 62.
Ingredients
5kg/11lb acidic apples
2.5kg/5lb sweet apples
2.5kg/5lb bitter apples
3 star anise
6 cinnamon sticks
8 cloves
Yeast

Add all the spices to the fermenter at the start of fermentation. If possible, transfer them for the first couple of rackings to infuse the flavours. In addition, you can add a star anise and a cinnamon stick per pint when warming the cider for drinking, as well as 1 dessertspoon of honey.

CHEAT'S CIDER

As the name suggests, this is a very fast way to make a cider-like drink out of season. It's also very easy to do, as if cider-making weren't easy enough already! I use a generic wine yeast for cheat's cider – nothing fancy. An ale yeast or even baker's yeast would do the job admirably.

Ingredients
4.5 litres/1 gallon/5 quarts apple juice (free from additives and sweeteners and not made from concentrate)
Yeast

Simply empty the juice into a demi-john, add the yeast and put in the bung and airlock. It's that simple! This doesn't need the maturing period of cider from apples, and can effectively be drunk straight from the demi-john. If you use cloudy apple juice, your cider will also be cloudy. If you leave it for months, it might clear, but it tastes just fine when it is cloudy.

MEAD

This is a very simple recipe which you can use as a basis for any experiments: add elderflowers, spices, or fruits – or simply have it as is. The price of honey has varied in the past, affecting the amount that people used in their mead recipe; as a result, other ingredients were sometimes used to make up the shortfall of honey. There are a number of variations on straight mead (which strictly has only honey, water and yeast) through to spiced mead or metheglin, cyser, braggot and melomels. Again, any of these recipes can be used as a base and you can add spices, flowers or other fruits to the mix. The recipes need not be followed slavishly: use them to provide you with inspiration. Mead is slightly higher in alcohol content than cider and beer. Treat it like wine, as it can be really quite strong, and can lead to an aggressive hangover. (Not that I'd know anything about that!)

Follow the process starting on page 66.

Ingredients

4.5 litres/1 gallon/5 quarts water

1.2kg/2½lb/scant 3½ cups honey

1 tsp yeast nutrient

Yeast

METHEGLIN

This is a basic spiced mead, or metheglin. The tea is used to add some astringency and body to the mead. You could adjust this to use any spices that you like: cinnamon or star anise are favourites, but you could easily use cumin or coriander seed. The ginger should be smashed up as much as possible, and the skin left on. This is because the fiery part of the ginger is just below the skin and peeling it can remove this.

Follow the process starting on page 62.
Ingredients
4.5 litres/1 gallon/5 quarts water
1.2kg/2½lb/scant 3½ cups honey
15 cloves
5cm/2in piece of ginger root, pulverised with skin on
300ml/½ pint/1¼ cups strong tea
1 tsp yeast nutrient
Yeast

BRAGGOT

This is a basic braggot, made by adding malt to the mead to make up some of the sugar in place of the honey. If most of the sugar comes from honey, the drink is called a braggot; if most of the sugar comes from malt, it's a honey beer. This has a hop addition. Add this to the water with the dried malt extract and boil for 15 minutes. Then leave the wort to cool and incorporate the honey when the water is below 75°C/167°F.

Follow the process starting on page 62.
Ingredients
4.5 litres/1 gallon/5 quarts water
750g/1lb 10oz/2⅛ cups honey
500g/1lb 2oz dried malt extract
30g/1oz Fuggle hops (or other aroma hop or dual-purpose hops; see Beer section)

CYSER

A melomel is a blend between honey as the source of fermentable sugar and a fruit juice. Cyser uses apple juice. This is a mix of sugars from apple juice and honey. The apple juice used in this recipe is assumed to have an OG of 1055 before being mixed with the rest of the water and honey. If you have less than a demi-john of apple juice left over from a pressing of cider, cyser is a good use for it.

Follow the process starting on page 62.

Ingredients

2.25 litres/4 pints/2⅜ quarts water

900g/2lb/generous 2½ cups honey

2.25 litres/4 pints/2½ quarts apple juice (freshly pressed, or free from additives and sweeteners and not made from concentrate)

1 tsp yeast nutrient

Yeast

PYMENT

This is a melomel made from a mixture of honey and grape juice. Again, much of the sugar in this recipe comes from honey. Alternatively, you could try melon juice, sloes, gooseberries or blackcurrants. The recipe uses grape concentrate, which can be obtained from home brew suppliers. However, if you are lucky enough to be pressing grapes for wine, and have less than a demi-john left over, use this as the basis for a pyment. Just top up with water and add honey until you reach the appropriate gravity.

Follow the process starting on page 62.
Ingredients
4 litres/7 pints/1 US gallon water
800g/1¾lb/2⅓ cups honey
500ml/16fl oz/generous 2 cups grape concentrate
1 tsp yeast nutrient
Yeast

FAMILY FAVOURITES

cordials, syrups and squashes

WHY MAKE YOUR OWN?

The advantages of making drinks at home for your family are numerous. Less sweet and heavy than most shop-bought varieties, they will also be free from artificial colours and flavourings. They taste better too and, of course, are much cheaper, especially if you use wild fruits and plants.

For centuries, most countrywomen made non-alcoholic fruit cordials, or syrups. (The two words mean the same thing except in the United States, where a cordial refers to a fruit-flavoured liqueur.) These usually found their place in the medicine cupboard to ease sore throats and ward off winter colds. They are also wonderful diluted with still or sparkling water and served ice-cold to quench thirst and restore stamina on a hot summer's day, or served steaming hot to warm you up after a brisk walk in the snow. They also preserve the nutritive properties of fruits, so are especially suitable for children.

Fruit cordials and syrups are concentrated and a little goes a long way, so they are economical when made in quantity. Undiluted, they are useful as cold or hot sauces for steamed and milk puddings, for pouring over ice cream and yoghurt, for sweet and sour sauces and for adding to casseroles and gravies. They can also be diluted to make jellies.

The recipes in this chapter do not include any heat treatments nor do they contain sufficient sugar to allow for long storage, so they should be drunk straight away, or kept in the refrigerator for just 3–4 weeks. Alternatively, the cordials and syrups can easily be frozen in small plastic containers, or in convenient quantities in ice-cube trays. Pour in the drink, leaving room for it to expand. When frozen, store the cubes in plastic bags in the freezer. One ice cube will be enough for a drink of 250ml/9fl oz/1 cup.

> ✳ HELPFUL HINT ✳
> If you can't find unwaxed lemons, preferably organic, use standard ones, but scrub the skins well with hot water to remove the wax coating before using.

FRESH LEMONADE

Home-made lemonade is one of the greatest pleasures of summer. It was actually a French invention, but some drinkers liked to add an equal quantity of white wine to make it rather more heady! This is a quick and easy recipe, using whole lemons. It can be used for any citrus fruit.

Ingredients

3 large unwaxed lemons

50–75g/1¾–2¾oz/¼ to generous ⅓ cup sugar

About 900ml/1½ pints/1 quart boiling water

Scrub the lemons, then slice up roughly and purée them coarsely in a food processor or blender, adding 300ml/½ pint/1¼ cups of water and 25g/1oz/2 tbsp of the sugar. Strain through a nylon sieve, then repeat the process twice more, using the pulp remaining in the sieve. Add extra water and sugar to taste.

Cover and chill well for 1–2 hours, then pour into a jug and serve with a few mint or lemon balm leaves, lemon slices and ice cubes. (Borage flowers also look very pretty.) This lemonade should be drunk within a few days. Store in the refrigerator.

MINT LEMONADE

Lemon and mint are a refreshing combination and make a cooling picnic drink. It should be drunk within a few days.

Ingredients

3 large unwaxed lemons

A generous handful of fresh mint leaves

2–3 tablespoons caster sugar

600ml/1 pint/20fl oz boiling water

Lightly crush the mint leaves and place in a heat-proof bowl with the sugar. Scrub the lemons, slice roughly, then purée coarsely in a food processor. Add this purée to the mint and pour in the boiling water. Cover and set aside for 1–2 hours, until cool. Strain through a nylon sieve into a jug. Serve with lemon slices, sprigs of mint and ice cubes. Store in the refrigerator

VARIATION

Burnet Lemonade

The leaves of the herb salad burnet have a fresh, cucumber-like taste, ideal for wine cups and cooling summer drinks. Use 2 tablespoons chopped salad burnet leaves instead of mint.

LEMON CORDIAL

Unlike fresh lemonade, this cordial can be stored for about 1 month in the refrigerator. Alternatively, you can pour it into clean plastic milk or juice cartons and freeze it. You can use other citrus fruits or a mixture of citrus fruits. Limes are particularly delicious.

Ingredients
3 large unwaxed lemons
900ml/1½ pints/1 quart boiling water
850g/1lb 14oz/4¼ cups white sugar
25g/1oz/2 tbsp citric or tartaric acid

Scrub the fruit well, then use a potato peeler to cut thick ribbons of rind from it, leaving the white pith behind. Place the rind in a heatproof bowl and pour the boiling water over it. Stir in the sugar until it has all dissolved.

Leave the mixture to cool for 1–2 hours, then add the juice from the lemons and the citric or tartaric acid. Cover and leave to steep overnight.

Next day, strain through a nylon sieve. (Don't leave the rind in any longer, or the cordial will become bitter.) Pour the strained cordial into 2 x 750ml/1¼ pint/3 cup sterilized, screw-top bottles or plastic cartons, then seal.

To serve, pour a little cordial into a glass and top up with still or sparkling water, or tonic water. Add ice and a slice of lemon. (This is also very good diluted with hot water, especially if you have a cold or flu.)

LEMONGRASS CORDIAL

Lemongrass stems, mixed with fresh ginger and lemon juice, make a delicious, thirst-quenching summer drink. It will keep for up to 1 month in the refrigerator or it can be frozen in plastic milk or juice containers. (Lemongrass is readily available at most supermarkets.)

Ingredients
3 lemongrass stems
5cm/2in piece of fresh root ginger
450g/1lb/2¼ cups sugar
600ml/1 pint/2½ cups water
Juice of 3 large lemons

Chop the tops off the lemongrass and bruise the base of the stems with a steak mallet or rolling pin, then slice thinly. Peel the ginger with a potato peeler, then slice thinly. Put the lemongrass and ginger into a saucepan and heat gently with the sugar and water. Stir until the sugar has dissolved, then increase the heat and simmer for about 5 minutes. Remove from the heat, add the lemon juice, and then cover and leave until completely cold.

Strain through a nylon sieve into a 750ml/1¼ pint/3 cup sterilized, screw-top bottle and store in the refrigerator. Use plastic cartons, if you want to freeze.

To serve, pour a little cordial into a glass and top up with still or sparkling water, or tonic water. Add ice and a slice of lemon or lime. (This is also very good topped up with hot water as a winter drink.)

GINGERADE WITH MINT

This is a very simple recipe and makes a delicious refreshing drink on a hot summer's day. It needs to be drunk more or less straight away, as it won't keep more than a few days.

Ingredients

A generous handful of fresh mint leaves, chopped
Grated zest of 2 large unwaxed lemons
2 tablespoons peeled and grated fresh root ginger
1 litre/1¾ pints/1 quart boiling water
3 tablespoons sugar

Put the mint, lemon zest and ginger in a heatproof bowl and pour in the boiling water. Add the sugar and stir until it has completely dissolved.

Cover the bowl and allow to cool. Strain into a jug and serve chilled with plenty of ice and a few fresh mint leaves.

LEMON BARLEY WATER

Barley water was originally drunk as a medicine, but later became the drink of genteel ladies. It is forever linked with tennis and croquet parties.

Ingredients
100g/3½oz/⅔ cups pearl barley
50g/2oz white sugar cubes
4 large lemons
1.2 litres/2 pints/1¼ quarts boiling water

Rinse the pearl barley in a sieve under cold running water and drain well. Place in a pan and pour in cold water to cover, then bring to the boil. Reduce the heat and cook gently for 5 minutes. Pour into a sieve and rinse again, then put in a large jug or bowl.

Rub each sugar cube over the lemons to extract their oils, then add the cubes to the barley. Pour in the boiling water and stir until the sugar has dissolved. Cover with a clean cloth and leave to infuse for 3 hours, or until cold.

Squeeze the juice from the lemons, then add it to the barley water and strain through a nylon sieve. Cover and chill for at least 1 hour before serving with plenty of ice and lemon slices. This needs to be drunk more or less straight away, as it will not keep well.

VARIATION

Lime Barley Water
Substitute 6–8 limes (depending on size) for the lemons.

ORANGE SQUASH

This is really a cordial and will keep in the refrigerator for 1 month, or it can be frozen in plastic cartons.

Ingredients
3 large thin-skinned oranges
1 large unwaxed lemon
1.2 litres/2 pints/1¼ quarts water
450g/1lb/2¼ cups sugar
25g/1oz/2 tbsp citric or tartaric acid

Scrub and dry the fruit, then squeeze out the juice and reserve. Remove all the pips and discard, then chop the fruit in a food processor. Turn the resulting pulp into a saucepan and add the water. Bring to the boil, then simmer for about 5 minutes.

Strain the liquid into a heatproof jug and stir in the sugar until completely dissolved. Cover and allow to cool, then add the reserved juice and the citric acid. Pour into sterilized screw-top bottles, seal, then store in the refrigerator.

To serve, dilute with still or sparkling water, tonic or soda water and serve with ice and orange slices.

GINGER BEER

This is my idea of the perfect drink for a summer party.

Ingredients
1 large unwaxed lemon
450g/1lb/2¼ cups sugar
1½ teaspoons cream of tartar
25g/1oz dried root ginger or 1 tablespoon ground ginger
4.5 litres/8 pints/4¾ quarts boiling water
25g/1oz fresh yeast or 1 tablespoon dried yeast

This is an excellent, speedy recipe for ginger beer. The drink is ready after 3 days and at this point it should be drunk as soon as possible before it explodes and the smell of ginger pervades the house! So, make it only for a special occasion when you need a large amount, like a children's party or picnic. Look out for recipes using ginger beer in case you have some over – ginger beer scones are delicious.

Scrub the lemon well, then pare off the rind thinly with a potato peeler. Remove all the white pith from the lemon and discard. Cut the lemon flesh into thin slices, removing and discarding the pips. Put the lemon rind and lemon slices into a large, heatproof bowl or clean plastic bucket with the sugar and cream of tartar. Bruise the root ginger with a steak mallet or rolling pin and add to the bowl. (If using ground ginger, just sprinkle it into the bowl with the cream of tartar.) Pour in the boiling water, then stir well. Leave until tepid, then add the yeast.

Cover and leave in a warm place for 24 hours to ferment. Skim off the froth with a slotted spoon, then strain through a muslin-lined nylon sieve. Pour into sterilized glass bottles with pop-off plastic caps (or plastic screw-capped bottles) in case of explosions!

Leave in a cool, dark place for 2–3 days before drinking, checking every day to make sure that the ginger beer is not too fizzy. If using glass bottles, be sure to release the caps slightly every day to let out any gas that may build up during fermentation and cause the bottles to explode. Drink within the week, well chilled.

VARIATION

Mulled Ginger Beer

Heat a bottle of ginger beer very gently in a saucepan with the thinly pared rind of 1 large orange, 4 whole cloves, a 5cm/2in piece of cinnamon stick and a pinch of ground mace. Bring slowly to simmering point, then continue simmering for 5–10 minutes. Strain into a heatproof jug and leave to cool a little before pouring into warmed glasses. Serve with an orange slice in each glass.

BERRY FIZZ

This pink strawberry syrup makes a pretty, cooling, fizzy drink and is an excellent sauce for ice cream and milk puddings.

Ingredients
1.5kg/3lb 5oz fresh, ripe strawberries
White sugar (see method)
Juice of 2 lemons

Hull the strawberries and purée them in a food processor. Line a nylon sieve with a double layer of muslin and strain the strawberry pulp through it into a non-metallic bowl. Gather the corners of the muslin and squeeze lightly to extract all the juice possible.

Measure the juice and for each 600ml/1 pint/2½ cups juice, weigh out 350g/12oz/1¾ cups sugar. Pour the juice into a saucepan, add the sugar and stir over a low heat until the sugar has completely dissolved. Stir in the lemon juice and cool for 5 minutes.

Pour into warm, sterilized bottles with screw-caps. Seal the bottles and leave to cool completely. Store in the refrigerator – it will keep for 3–4 weeks, or freeze in plastic containers. To serve, pour some syrup into each glass, add ice cubes and top up with soda water.

VARIATION

Other strongly acidic fruits such as raspberries, cloudberries and loganberries can be used instead of strawberries.

ELDERFLOWER CORDIAL

Now one of the most popular bases for soft drinks, this cordial is easy to make and tastes far better than shop-bought variations. Use it to flavour ice creams, fools and fruit salads. Pick the flowers on a dry, sunny day, when they are almost in full bloom.

Ingredients

About 15 large elderflower heads
1kg/2¼lb/4 cups white sugar
850ml/1½ pints/1¾ US pints boiling water
40g/1½oz/scant ¼ cup citric acid
2 lemons, sliced

Put the sugar into a large, heatproof bowl and pour in the boiling water. Stir until the sugar has dissolved, then stir in the citric acid. Ensuring they are insect-free, snip the individual flowers from their stems and add to the bowl with the sliced lemons. Cover the bowl with a clean cloth and leave to stand for 5 days, stirring daily.

Strain through a nylon sieve, lined with muslin, into a jug, then pour into small, sterilized, screw-top bottles. Seal and store in the refrigerator – it will keep for up to 3 months, or pour into plastic bottles and freeze.

To serve, dilute with still or sparkling water, soda or tonic water, and garnish with extra lemon slices, tiny sprigs of lemon balm, if available, a few fresh elderflowers and plenty of ice.

LOGANBERRY AND LEMON BALM CORDIAL

Raspberries or cloudberries can be used instead: experiment with flavours of your choice or make use of any seasonal gluts.

Ingredients
1.8kg/4lb fresh or frozen loganberries
6 sprigs of fresh lemon balm
600ml/1 pint/2½ cups water
White sugar (see method)
Juice of 2 lemons

Pick over the loganberries, discarding any leaves, but don't wash them. Put into a large saucepan with the lemon balm and the water. Bring slowly to the boil, then simmer over a low heat for about 10 minutes, or until the fruit is soft. Mash the pulp with a potato masher.

Line a nylon sieve with a double layer of muslin, then strain the pulp through it into a non-metallic bowl. Gather the corners of the muslin and squeeze lightly to extract all the juice possible.

Measure the juice and for each 600ml/1 pint/2½ cups, weigh out 225g/8oz/1⅛ cups sugar. Pour the juice back into the saucepan, add the sugar and stir over a low heat until the sugar has completely dissolved. Stir in the lemon juice. Bring the mixture to the boil, then simmer for 5 minutes. Cool for 5 minutes, then pour into warm, sterilized, screw-cap bottles. Seal and leave to cool completely. Serve chilled, diluted with still or sparkling water and with a sprig of fresh lemon balm in each glass.

Store in the refrigerator – it will keep for about 1 month, or freeze in plastic containers. (This is also good as a warming winter drink, diluted with boiling water.)

CITRON PRESSE

Served in every French and Italian café, where you add sugar to taste to your own glass. In this version, sugar is added when you make the drink.

Ingredients
225g/8oz/1⅛ cups caster sugar
850ml/1½ pints/3¾ cups water
400ml/14fl oz/scant 1¾ cups freshly squeezed lemon juice (from 12–14 lemons)

Gently dissolve the sugar in the water over a low heat, then leave to cool.

Stir in the lemon juice, then chill well. Serve with ice, lemon slices and mint leaves.

ST CLEMENT'S CORDIAL

A friend was kind enough to give me this recipe years ago. She frequently won prizes for it in local agricultural shows and I still can't better it.

Ingredients
4 large juicy oranges
2 lemons
900g/2lb/4½ cups sugar
1.2 litres/2 pints/1¼ quarts boiling water
25g/1oz/2 tbsp citric acid
15g/½oz/1 tbsp tartaric acid

Process the fruit coarsely and place in a large, heatproof bowl. Add the sugar and boiling water. Stir well until the sugar has completely dissolved. Cover with a clean cloth and leave to steep for 24 hours.

Next day, stir in the citric and tartaric acids. Strain at least three times through a nylon sieve, then pour into 2 x 750ml/1¼ pint/3 cup sterilized, screw-top bottles. Seal tightly, then store in the refrigerator: it will keep for up to 1 month. Dilute to taste with still or sparkling water and serve chilled with orange slices, a few sprigs of lemon balm and borage flowers, if available.

PINEAPPLE AND LIME CORDIAL

This tropical-tasting cordial makes a wonderful base for rum punch or a daiquiri. Alternatively, serve it diluted with sparkling mineral water as a cooling, non-alcoholic drink.

Ingredients
2 ripe pineapples (about 2kg/4lb)
300ml/½ pint/1¼ cups water
About 175g/6oz/scant 1 cup sugar
Juice of 3 limes

Slice the tops off the pineapples and cut off the peel, cutting deep enough to remove the 'eyes'. Slice the pineapple and cut out and discard the hard central core from each slice. Finely chop the flesh, then place in a saucepan with the water. Bring slowly to the boil, then simmer over a low heat for about 20 minutes, or until the fruit is soft and pulpy. Mash the pulp with a potato masher. Line a nylon sieve with a double layer of muslin. Strain the pineapple pulp through the muslin into a non-metallic bowl. Gather the corners of the muslin and squeeze lightly to extract all the juice possible. Discard the pulp, then measure the juice. For each 300ml/½ pint/1¼ cups juice, weigh out 100g/3½oz/½ cup sugar.

Pour the juice back into the saucepan, add the sugar and stir over a low heat until the sugar has dissolved completely. Stir in the lime juice. Bring the mixture slowly to the boil and simmer over a low heat for 5 minutes. Cool for 5 minutes, then pour into warm, sterilized, screw-capped bottles. Seal and leave until cold before storing in the refrigerator.

Drink within 3–4 weeks, diluted with sparkling mineral water or soda water. Serve with lots of ice and twists of orange or lime peel for added zip.

BLACKBERRY AND APPLE CORDIAL

You can make your own apple juice or buy a good, farm-pressed juice for this delicious autumnal drink, which I like to drink hot, but do try it chilled as well.

Ingredients

1.8kg/4lb fresh or frozen blackberries
600ml/1 pint/2½ cups apple juice
Sugar (see method)
Juice of 2 lemons

Pick over the blackberries and if fresh, wash briefly and dry. Put in a large saucepan with the apple juice. Bring to the boil and simmer over a very low heat for 20 minutes, or until the fruit is soft. Mash the pulp with a potato masher. Line a nylon sieve with a double layer of muslin, then strain the pulp through it into a non-metallic bowl.

Gather the corners of the muslin and squeeze lightly to extract as much juice as possible. Measure the juice and for each 600ml/1 pint/2½ cups, weigh out 225g/8oz/1⅛ cups sugar. Pour the juice back into the saucepan with the sugar. Stir over a low heat until the sugar has completely dissolved, then stir in the lemon juice. Bring the mixture to the boil, then simmer gently for about 5 minutes.

Cool for another 5 minutes, then pour into warm, sterilized, screw-capped bottles, or plastic containers if you are planning to freeze, and seal.

Store in the refrigerator, where it will keep for up to 1 month. Dilute with still or sparkling water and serve chilled, or with boiling water if you want to serve it hot.

ROSEHIP SYRUP

Pick the largest rosehips you can find – the fruit of *Rosa rugosa* is ideal because it is very juicy – and use as soon as possible to maximize the vitamin C content. Rosehips may irritate the skin, so wear protective gloves to process them.

Try this slightly scented syrup diluted with boiling water as a soothing drink when you have a cold, or drizzle over meringues, ice cream, milk puddings and hot steamed puddings, or use as a base for a fresh fruit salad.

Ingredients
900g/2lb ripe rosehips
2.5 litres/4½ pints/10 cups cold water
450g/1lb/2¼ cups sugar

Wash and dry the rosehips, then chop roughly by hand or coarsely in a food processor. Place in a large saucepan with 1.7 litres/3 pints/7 cups of the water and bring slowly to the boil. Remove from the heat, cover the pan and leave to infuse for about 20 minutes, then strain through a jelly bag, or a nylon sieve lined with a double layer of muslin, over a bowl. Reserve the juice and return the pulp to the saucepan, adding the remaining water. Bring to the boil, then cover and set aside for 20 minutes, as before. Strain this juice as before.

Pour the strained liquids into a clean saucepan and bring to the boil. Continue boiling gently until reduced to about 850ml/1½ pints/3¾ cups. Add the sugar, stirring until dissolved, then simmer for a further 10 minutes. Cool for a few minutes, then pour into small, warm, sterilized, screw-capped bottles. Seal, then cool completely. Store in the refrigerator, where the syrup will keep for about 1 month.

BLACKCURRANT SYRUP

Other fruits, such as cranberries, lingonberries, blueberries, bilberries, elderberries and whitecurrants can be used in this recipe. Redcurrants make rather an astringent syrup if used on their own; mix with raspberries or strawberries for a much better result.

Ingredients
900g/2lb fresh or frozen blackcurrants
300ml/½ pint/1¼ cups water
Sugar (see method)

Pick over the fruit and discard any that is damaged. Strip the berries from the stalks with a fork and wash them. Put in the top of a double saucepan, or in a bowl over a pan of simmering water. Bruise the fruit well with a wooden spoon, then heat gently with the water for about 1 hour until soft, pressing frequently with the spoon, to help release the juice. Strain through a jelly bag or a large nylon sieve lined with two layers of muslin and leave to drain overnight.

Next day, measure the strained juice and pour into a saucepan. For every 600ml/1 pint/2½ cups juice, add 350g/12oz/1¾ cups sugar. Stir over a low heat until the sugar has completely dissolved, then simmer for 15 minutes. Remove from the heat and allow to cool for a few minutes.

Pour into small, sterilized, screw-capped bottles and seal tightly. Store in the refrigerator: it will keep for up to 1 month.

Stir a spoonful of syrup into a glass of iced still or sparkling water for a refreshing summer drink, or dilute with boiling water for a warming drink in winter.

VARIATION

Elderberry Rob
Use elderberries instead of blackcurrants and make as before, using only 150ml/¼ pint/⅔ cup water. Stir 1 teaspoon honey and a pinch of ground cinnamon into a glass of hot water, then stir in 1–2 tablespoons elderberry syrup. This makes a lovely warming drink.

RASPBERRY CORDIAL

A pleasant nightcap, which is said to be good for relieving a cold. Replace the raspberries with cloudberries, loganberries, blackberries or strawberries for an equally delicious cordial.

Ingredients

450g/1lb/3 cups very ripe raspberries

600ml/1 pint/2½ cups wine vinegar or cider vinegar

Sugar (see method)

Pick over the raspberries and remove any leaves and stalks, but do not wash. Place in a large non-metallic bowl and break up the fruit a little with a wooden spoon. Pour in the vinegar and cover with a clean cloth. Leave in a sunny place, or airing cupboard, for 5–7 days, just stirring occasionally.

Strain through a jelly bag or through a nylon sieve lined with two layers of muslin. Leave to drain overnight.

Next day, measure the liquid. Weigh out the appropriate amount of sugar – 450g/1lb/2¼ cups to each 600ml/1 pint/2½ cups liquid – and place both in a saucepan. Heat gently until all the sugar has dissolved, then bring to the boil. Boil rapidly for 10 minutes, then cool a little.

Pour into small, sterilized, vinegar-proof, screw-capped bottles and seal tightly. Store in the refrigerator: it will keep for up to 1 month.

To serve, stir a spoonful into a glass of iced still or sparkling mineral water for a refreshing summer drink, or dilute with boiling water for a warming drink in winter. Undiluted, this cordial makes a wonderful sweet and sour sauce for stir-fries and casseroles, and for adding to gravies to accompany lamb, duck and game.

LAVENDER 'CHAMPAGNE'

A delicious, lightly scented and unusual fizzy drink for a hot summer's day. Make sure the lavender flowers have not been sprayed with insecticides and pesticides, and pick on a dry, sunny day.

Ingredients

40 heads fresh lavender flowers
300g/10½oz/1½ cups white sugar
100g/3½oz/generous ½ cup sultanas, finely chopped
2 litres/3½ pints/8 cups cold boiled water
2 tablespoons white wine vinegar
Juice of 1 lemon

Shake the flowers gently to remove any insects, then pick them from their stalks. Place in a large non-metallic bowl with the sugar and chopped sultanas. Stir the dry ingredients together, then pour in the water, wine vinegar and lemon juice. Stir again, then cover with clingfilm and leave for 7 days.

When ready, strain the liquid through a muslin-lined nylon sieve into a jug, then into strong, sterilized glass bottles with pop-off plastic caps, or plastic mineral water bottles with screw-caps.

Leave in a cool, dark place for another 7 days, by which time the liquid should be sparkling and ready to drink. Serve well chilled. Store in the refrigerator.

LAVENDER CORDIAL

A pleasantly refreshing and calming drink, with an exquisite aromatic flavour, which is perfect on a hot summer's day. As in the previous recipe, make sure the lavender flowers have not been sprayed with insecticides and pesticides.

Ingredients
300ml/½ pint/1¼ cups water
125g/4½oz/generous ½ cup white sugar
50 heads fresh lavender flowers

Put the water and sugar into a saucepan and heat gently until the sugar has dissolved completely. Shake the lavender flowers to remove any insects, then remove from their stalks. Add to the syrup. Bring to the boil, then remove from the heat, cover the pan and leave to infuse for 30–45 minutes.

Strain the liquid through a muslin-lined nylon sieve into another saucepan and bring back to the boil, stirring all the time until the mixture is reduced and syrupy. Take off the heat and cool completely. Pour into small, sterilized, screw-topped bottles. Seal tightly, then leave to become completely cold.

Store in the refrigerator until required, where the cordial will keep for 1 month. Dilute with chilled still or sparkling mineral water.

VARIATION

Champagne Lavender Cocktail

Pour 1½ teaspoons of lavender cordial into a champagne flute and top up with Champagne or good-quality sparkling white wine. Garnish with a fresh lavender sprig and serve as an apéritif, or for a toast, particularly at a summer wedding.

ELDERFLOWER FIZZ

Elderflower fizz, said to 'lift the heart and clear the blood of all impurities', has been a favourite summer drink with country people for years. It is light, fragrant and extremely fizzy and I am always amazed that such a superb drink can be made from such simple ingredients and in just three weeks. This recipe was given to me by an elderly lady living in my local village – a strict teetotaller. She insisted that it was non-alcoholic – I believed her!

Pick the flowers on a dry, sunny day when the elder blossom, and its perfume, are at their peak.

Ingredients

About 5 large, freshly gathered elderflower heads
700g/1lb 9oz/3½ cups white sugar
2 tablespoons white wine vinegar
1 large unwaxed lemon
4.6 litres/8 pints/4¾ quarts cold water

Shake the flower heads gently to remove any insects, then snip the flowers from their stalks into a large non-metallic bowl. (I use a lovely Victorian china washbowl, which has become part of the ritual and enjoyment of making elderflower champagne early in the summer each year.)

Add the sugar and wine vinegar. Thinly pare the rind from the lemon and squeeze out the juice, then add the other ingredients. Pour in the water, cover with a clean cloth and leave to steep for 24 hours.

Next day, strain through a muslin-lined nylon sieve into a jug, then pour into sterilized bottles with suitable caps. (Use strong beer bottles with pop-off caps, champagne bottles or fizzy drink bottles, preferably with old-fashioned wire stoppers. Plastic mineral water bottles or lemonade bottles with screw-tops also work well.)

Seal your chosen bottles firmly and allow to stand in a cool, dark place for about 2–3 weeks, at which point it will be strongly effervescent and ready to drink. Chill well before serving. Drink quickly once the champagne is ready, because its flavour will deteriorate rapidly.

Try pouring a little elderflower champagne over soft fruit such as strawberries and raspberries, or stone fruit, like peaches and apricots, just before serving.

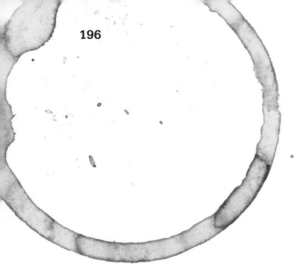

HELEN'S WINTER CORDIAL

When one of my friends gave me this recipe, I was struck by how much it resembled the old-fashioned country drink known as stokos, which was introduced into America and Britain in the 1880s by the temperance movement, to replace the beer and cider drunk by working people.

Although Helen's family drink this hot, I think it's good chilled, like the original stokos.

Ingredients

4 dessertspoons fine or medium oatmeal
2 dessertspoons demerara sugar
½ teaspoon ground ginger
1 unwaxed lemon
1.2 litres/2 pints/1¼ quarts boiling water

Mix the oatmeal, sugar and ginger in a basin. Add the zest of the lemon, then gradually pour in the boiling water, stirring all the time.

Transfer to a saucepan, add the lemon juice and slowly bring to the boil. Simmer gently for 10 minutes, then strain and serve hot.

Helen uses the leftover oatmeal and lemon zest mixture to make a bread pudding.

(Also illustrated on previous page.)

TERMINOLOGY

ALPHA ACID OR AA

This is the part of hops which dictates how much bittering they will provide. It is expressed as a percentage, and is marked up on most packets of commercially available hops. Recipes in this book make assumptions about specific Alpha Acid levels (see hop table, page 48). If your hops differ from these, you will need to calculate how much more or less is required (see page 47).

BITTERNESS: IBU/EBU

This is an important part of the taste profile of any beer, and the addition of hops contributes directly to this. There are two units for measuring this: the international Bitterness Unit (IBU) or the European Bitterness Unit (EBU). Since they refer to the exact same thing, they can be used interchangeably. There are a number of formulas for predicting the bitterness level of a recipe. This book use the Daniels formula.

BREW LENGTH

When brewers talk about the amount of beer they are going to end up with, they refer to the brew 'length' (despite the fact that it is clearly a volume). The recipes in this book are all designed for a brew length of 23 litres /40 pints/6 US gallons.

COLD BREAK

This is similar to the hot break (see overleaf), but occurs while the wort is cooling down: yet more proteins clump together and begin to fall out of suspension.

COLOUR: EBC/SRM

The colour of a beer is measured on one of two scales, ranging from light straw/yellow lagers through to dark black/ruby coloured stouts. The European Beer Colour (EBC) is most used in Europe and Standard Reference Method (SRM) is more often used in the United States. There are a number of different formulas for predicting the colour of a recipe. This book uses the Morey formula.

COPPER

This is another name for the boiler, though no boilers are made of copper anymore. The term is still relevant today because brewers talk about copper finings. These are not made of copper but are meant for use in the boiler.

DECOCTION

This is an advanced technique used to intensify the malt flavours in lighter beers such as lagers. It involves pulling out part of the mash and boiling it for a period of time, then returning to the mash. This can be done a number of times, traditionally between 1 and 3 times.

EFFICIENCY

This describes how efficient a brewer's setup is. It depends on many factors, including the crush of the grain, the loss of liquor due to mash tun or boiler design, and the absorption of the wort by the hops. Many experienced brewers calculate this to ensure that they can make accurate predictions about their beers. The recipes in this book assume an efficiency of around 75%, which should be achievable by all home brewers.

FININGS

Finings are used to promote clarity in beer. These can be added to the boil (copper finings) or later in the process. Most copper finings are based on Irish Moss, a type of seaweed. Other products such as gelatine and isinglass are also used later in the process.

GRAIN BILL

This is the total of all the grains used in the mash. Quite often discussed in terms of large grain bills or small grain bills.

HOT LIQUOR TANK OR HLT

In home brewing, the boiler normally stands in for an HLT. In more complex systems, a separate tank is used to heat the treated water prior to the mash. This can be really useful, allowing water from the mash to go straight into the boiler.

HOT BREAK

This is a part of the process of heating the water to boiling point. Once the wort has been heated/boiled for a time, some of the proteins from the grain start to clump together and drop out of suspension in the wort. It manifests as a slightly stringy texture in the boil.

LAGERING

This is the process that gives us the name lager. Derived from the German word for larder, it refers to the maturing of the beer at low temperatures. It is an important part of creating genuine lager styles of beer, alongside the use of lager yeast. This can be difficult for home brewers to achieve, and is one of the reasons that most home brewers brew ales, which do not require this process.

LAUTERING OR SPARGING

These are both terms for the process of washing out the sugar from the grain after the mashing process. There are subtle differences between the two terms, but in home brewing contexts they tend to be used interchangeably.

LIQUOR

This is the water that has been prepared for use in brewing, either by water treatment processes as outlined on page 48 or simply by being set aside for use.

MASHING

This is the process of extracting the sugars from the grain. Hot water is added to the crushed grain (or grist) and left to mash over a period of time. The different temperatures and time periods will give different amounts of sugar and character in the beer.

MATURING

This is the latter part of the conditioning process for beers. The first part, the secondary fermentation, carbonates the beer, adding the fizz where required. The maturing allows the flavours to develop, creating the final taste of the beer.

STRIKE WATER

This is the water that has been heated to the right temperature (the strike temperature) to add to the grist, in order to bring the mash to the mashing temperature – often higher than the mash temperature by 8–10°C/46–50°F, to allow for heat loss from the grain and the mash tun.

TRUB

Once the boiler has been drained, the debris left in the bottom is the trub. This will contain a combination of coagulated proteins and rehydrated hops. This is best put on the compost heap. The same word is sometimes used to describe the cake of yeast left in the bottom of the fermenter. This can be reused, composted, or processed into a yeast spread you will either love or hate.

WORT

Once the liquor has been used to sparge the mash, the resultant water coming out (full of sugar) is called the wort, or sweet wort (pronounced 'wert').

INDEX

THANKS!

DOUG

I would like to thank my wife and children for their patience without which I would never have finished writing this. Thanks to Dave for asking questions and being my partner in brewing crime, to Nev for reading and questioning what I had written. Thanks to Mark (as well as Dave, Nev and others) for testing and sampling what was produced and acting as quality control on the final products. I'd like to thank Paul at Barley Bottom for being a fantastic grain and hop supplier, and finally, thanks very much to Katie for getting me involved in this project and to all the people at Anova who have contributed and shaped it into what it is.

SARA

A big thank you must go to so many Cornish friends who over the last 35 years have generously shared family favourites with me. One particularly special friend's expertise in country wine-making has always inspired me to have another go when my results have not been quite as expected! Huge thanks as well to another special person, Barbara Magor, who, with so little fuss, transferred my 'enthusiastic' manuscript into an orderly and readable collection of recipes.

First published in Great Britain in 2010 by
Pavilion Books
Old West London Magistrates Court
10 Southcombe Street
London, W14 0RA

An imprint of the Anova Books Company Ltd

Design and layout © Pavilion, 2010
Text © Sara Paston-Williams and Doug Rouxel
Photography © Diana Miller

Publisher: Anna Cheifetz
Project editor: Katie Deane
Senior Designer (and cover illustration): Georgina Hewitt
Production Manager: Oliver Jeffreys
Copy editor: Caroline Curtis
Proofreader: Fiona Corbridge
Photographer: Diana Miller
Photographer's Assistant: Danielle Wood
Stylist: Wei Tang
Indexer: Sandra Shotter

ISBN 978-1-86205-882-8

A CIP catalogue record for this book is available from the British Library.

10 9 8 7 6 5 4 3 2 1

Reproduction by Mission Productions Limited, Hong Kong
Printed and bound by Times Offset, Malaysia

www.anovabooks.com